Why
Niebuhr
Now?

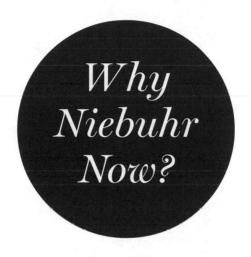

Why Niebuhr Now?

JOHN PATRICK DIGGINS

THE UNIVERSITY OF CHICAGO PRESS

Chicago & London

JOHN PATRICK DIGGINS (1935–2009) was distinguished professor at the City University of New York and the author of many books, including *Eugene O'Neill's America*, *The Promise of Pragmatism: Modernism and the Crisis of Knowledge and Authority*, *Ronald Reagan: Fate, Freedom, and the Making of History*, and *The Lost Soul of American Politics: Virtue, Self-Interest, and the Foundations of Liberalism*.

The University of Chicago Press, Chicago 60637
The University of Chicago Press, Ltd., London
© 2011 by The University of Chicago
All rights reserved. Published 2011
Printed in the United States of America

20 19 18 17 16 15 14 13 12 11   1 2 3 4 5

ISBN-13: 978-0-226-14883-0   (cloth)
ISBN-10: 0-226-14883-1   (cloth)

Library of Congress Cataloging-in-Publication Data

Diggins, John P.
Why Niebuhr now? / John Patrick Diggins.
p. cm.
Includes bibliographical references and index.
ISBN-13: 978-0-226-14883-0 (hardcover : alk. paper)
ISBN-10: 0-226-14883-1 (hardcover : alk. paper)
1. Niebuhr, Reinhold, 1892–1971.   2. Religion and civilization.
3. Religion and politics.   I. Title.
BX4827.N5D54 2011
230'.044092—dc22

2010048739

♾ The paper used in this publication meets the minimum requirements of the American National Standard for Information Sciences—Permanence of Paper for Printed Library Materials, ANSI Z39.48-1992.

Contents

Foreword

BY ROBERT HUBERTY

In more than a dozen books and several hundred articles and reviews, Jack Diggins tested the truth of ideas against one another and against the power of self-interest. In studies of American political ideas, from John Adams and Abraham Lincoln to the modern American Left and Right, and in his work on pragmatism, the sociology of Thorstein Veblen and Max Weber, and the plays of Eugene O'Neill, Diggins asked what we can know and whether what we know helps us to live with others—and with ourselves. *Why Niebuhr Now?* is a natural progression in this intellectual project and a fitting conclusion to a distinguished career.

For Diggins it was not enough to put ideas in historical context, tracing their antecedents and consequences. He was unembarrassed about wanting to know whether our ideas are true and good, and what results from them. What otherwise was the point of intellectual history?

Diggins's own context was his rebellious Catholic boyhood in working-class San Francisco. In the preface to his book *On Hallowed Ground: Abraham Lincoln and the Foundations of American History* (2000), he wrote, "In the early 1950s I lost my faith and

found my mind." "As an ex-Catholic," he explained, "I have no quarrel with being told that the religious beliefs I once held were simply
a matter of the circumstances of my birth. But I do have a problem with schools of thought that claim we can get along without
the authority of truth." This outlook informs Diggins's meditation
on Reinhold Niebuhr and shapes his assessment of the theologian's
commentaries on religion and society.

In *Why Niebuhr Now?* Diggins focuses on a thinker whose ideas
permeate many of his books but who had never received his concentrated attention. Diggins completed the manuscript shortly
before his death on January 28, 2009. Elizabeth Harlan, his com-
panion and literary executor, asked me to review the text, to check
facts and footnotes, fill in narrative chinks, and buff away syntactic
rough edges. As his former graduate student at the University of
California, Irvine, and a friend of forty years, I was honored to assist her.

As with any posthumous publication, readers may question
whether the author would have "signed off" on the final product.
Some sections of this book might have benefited from greater discussion or more detail; illness kept Diggins from conducting the
additional research he intended at the Library of Congress, where
Niebuhr's papers are housed. And undoubtedly there are matters he
would have revisited, as was his habit, right up to publication.

My principal revision to the manuscript has been to reposition
what Diggins labeled a "preface" as the study's final chapter. A com-
pressed and complex essay, it begins with a deliberately provocative
but carefully considered title, "God Is Dead—Long Live Religion!"
The phrase is a paradoxical response to a Nietzschean quip by Eugene O'Neill, "God Is Dead! Long Live—What?," which Diggins
cites in the concluding chapter of his groundbreaking study *Eugene
O'Neill's America: Desire under Democracy*, published in 2007. In
that book, Diggins examines the anguished Irish-American dramatist, whose tragic characters dream and strive only to be broken by
the burden of their history. In O'Neill's plays "the mind is bonded to
the self and its desires," writes Diggins. "You are who you were."

The historian John Patrick Diggins understood that men and women are creatures of history, but he knew that they are also its creators. In his sympathetic reflections on the theologian Reinhold Niebuhr you may find an answer to the question posed by his title: *Why Niebuhr Now?*

Acknowledgments

My late partner, John Patrick Diggins, had been preoccupied with thoughts about Reinhold Niebuhr for many years, but the courage and conviction to write a book about this much admired figure only came to Jack in the twilight of his life, when most of his major work had been completed.

When Jack died in January of 2009, of complications from the colon cancer with which he had been diagnosed eighteen months before, drafts of *Why Niebuhr Now?* were scattered over four computers stored in several homes and at his office at the Graduate Center of the City University of New York. President William Kelly was unstinting in making available whatever resources were needed to set in order the intellectual legacy of his late colleague and good friend.

With the generous help of Ben Persky, a graduate student assigned to assist with electronic files, a unified manuscript of Jack's final work was assembled. Ben's exceptional technical skills were not the only gift he gave. In the months immediately succeeding Jack's death, Ben's capable and calming presence as he went about decoding, dating, and correlating multiple editions of Jack's numerous and expansive drafts, steadied me and raised hope that this project would see the light of day.

To prepare the manuscript for submission, I turned to Jack's former student Robert Huberty. Bob was, Jack wrote in a 1974 letter of recommendation, "*the* best graduate student I have had . . . and in certain matters involving theoretical reflection and speculation, he is one of the sharpest persons I have ever known." A mentor relationship was succeeded by a deep and enduring bond. As Jack's oeuvre grew and gathered, Bob frequently read and critiqued his work in progress, and I'm aware of no one whose opinion and discretion Jack honored more.

I would be remiss not to include here my thanks to Bob's partner, David Lott. As Bob read Jack, David often read over Bob's shoulder and offered astute suggestions based on his own professional connection with theological scholarship.

It so happens that living with a man for fifteen years gives one access to privileged information. Among the many distinguished editors with whom Jack worked over the course of his remarkably fecund career, Doug Mitchell is the intellectual figure for whom he felt the strongest affinity. At the 2009 meeting of the American Historical Association, which convened in New York at the top of the new year, just weeks before he died, Jack approached Doug with the request that he consider his book on Reinhold Niebuhr for publication by University of Chicago Press. I take this opportunity to express my gratitude for Doug's sensitive, respectful, and loyal response; there could be no more fitting final resting place for Jack's *opus ultimum*.

Elizabeth Harlan

Introduction:
What We Can Learn from
Reinhold Niebuhr

In 1939 Reinhold Niebuhr was selected to deliver the renowned Gifford Lectures at the University of Edinburgh. The annual series aims to promote the study of natural theology, the knowledge of God, and if the theme is meant to be profound, the setting that year was ominous. In October many of those listening to Niebuhr's second set of lectures in the university's Rainy Hall shuddered in dread. Not only was his theme, "The Nature and Destiny of Man," darkly foreboding, but during one lecture the roar of antiaircraft guns could be heard responding to a Luftwaffe attack on British ships docked in a nearby harbor.

During the next two years Great Britain would stand almost alone against Nazi Germany while an isolationist America watched nervously from distant shores. Western Europe capitulated to Nazi forces, and Hitler rained bombs on London, aiming to defeat Great Britain before abrogating his nonaggression pact with Joseph Stalin and turning east to conquer the Soviet Union. Niebuhr believed the West was intellectually as well as militarily unprepared to confront the menace of fascism, and he was deeply troubled as he surveyed the resources available to stand against Nazi Germany.

In many respects it seemed that the institutions of organized religion were as reluctant as Europe's democratic governments to firmly oppose tyranny. The Roman Catholic Church had adopted a strategy of accommodation. Relieved that the Black Shirts had saved Italy from communism, the Vatican negotiated the Lateran treaties with Benito Mussolini in 1929, securing its sovereignty and the church's status as Italy's state religion. In Germany the church protected itself with a *Reichskonkordat* worked out with Hitler's regime in 1933, and in Spain it sided with the Falangist movement and General Francisco Franco during the 1936 to 1939 civil war. "There is a peculiar pathos in the present anti-Communist campaign," wrote Niebuhr in 1939, "with its admission that the Church does not like Fascism but prefers it to Communism because Communism tries to destroy it while Fascism merely embarrasses it."[1]

The Protestant churches in America and Europe were mostly antifascist and anticommunist and committed to liberal democracy. But many were also antiwar, steeped in doctrines of nonviolence and injunctions to love your enemy and turn the other cheek. Niebuhr felt his challenge here was to affirm the Christian conscience while demonstrating that pacifism was dubious for religion and dangerous in politics. With Hitler on the march, he insisted that Protestants recall the "sinfulness of human nature" that obstructs the ethic of pure love. Humanity's goodness is an illusion that could not stop Nazi tyranny. The theologian even drew upon pagan sources to drive home his point: Sin is as inevitable in Christianity as tragedy is in Greek drama, and there is no escape when the human condition is oppressed by fate rather than liberated by freedom. "The history of our era seems to move in tragic circles strangely analogous to those presented symbolically in Greek tragedy," he wrote in 1938. "The democratic nations of the world are involving themselves more inexorably in world catastrophe by their very efforts to avert and avoid it. . . . Why are democratic nations so tragically committed to this dance of death?"[2]

As for Judaism, it was the most tragic of faiths, imperiled by the hopefulness of its theology. As a prophetic religion that envisions God as present in history, Judaism is self-affirming and life-enhancing and, indeed, the instrument of the world's redemption.

In Judaism there is no Fall of Man. Humankind may be alienated from Yahweh and liable to punishment, but the soul is not stained by original sin and the eternal damnation that requires a divine savior. Judaism is not ironic but messianic; a living God acts in history to help his people overcome adversity and find fulfillment in "the world to come," the Kingdom of God.[3]

All the more reason why Niebuhr grew alarmed about what was in store for the Jewish people at the time of the *Anschluss*, Germany's annexation of Austria in 1938:

> With the entrance of the Nazis into Vienna their anti-Semitic fury has reached new proportions. Here was a city in which Jewish intelligence played a significant role in the cultural achievements of the nation, particularly in medicine and music. The Nazis swooped down upon the city and wreaked indescribable terror. The Jews have been spared no indignity. . . . The tragic events since the taking of Austria allow us to see the racial fanaticism inherent in the Nazi creed in boldest outline. This is really the final destruction of every concept of universal values upon which Western civilization has been built.[4]

If traditional religion hesitated before the evil of fascism, modern thought appeared unable to recognize it. Disavowing the spiritual and the supernatural, intellectuals in the 1930s looked to science for a naturalistic explanation of events. But though theorists might explain war as an aggressive biological urge or identify fascism as advancing the interest of a social class, they were unprepared for the events of 1939.

The decade's touchstones of naturalism—the ideas of Marx, Freud, and Darwin—were of little use. Marxists who had joined the Communist Party were shameless in defending Moscow's nonaggression pact with Hitler and opposed America's entry into the war. Sigmund Freud's death that year meant there would be no guidance from the father of psychoanalysis, who had once claimed humanity carried a "death instinct." And America's leading Darwinian, the philosopher John Dewey, who championed scientific inquiry as an instrument of social reform, surveyed the outbreak of war in Europe and gave his country six words of advice: "No matter what happens, stay out!"[5] Even many of those adamantly opposed to fascism and revolted by the barbaric attacks on the Jews recoiled at the thought of going to war. Clearly modern thought needed a new voice.

When Reinhold Niebuhr came to prominence in the 1930s and 1940s, he warned that Christians would be tempted to invoke Jesus's Sermon on the Mount to justify refusing to take up arms against evil. In the face of the totalitarian threat, a religious aversion to violence seemed to him a delusionary conceit, the bad faith of a conscience trying selfishly to retain its innocence in an amoral and power-driven world.

Today the situation is different. At a Republican primary debate during the 2000 presidential election, Texas governor George W. Bush was asked to name the "philosopher" who most influenced his life. Bush replied, "Christ, because he changed my heart." The man who as president took America to war in Iraq thought Jesus was at his side. President Bush told reporter Bob Woodward that he sought counsel from "a higher father" on whether to go to war, and he delighted in saying with a cocky smile, "Bring 'em on." In our time the problem of religion is not its debilitating pacifism but its overbearing militarism. When "Mission Accomplished" adorned the tower of a US aircraft carrier in May 2003, genuine Christian humility was sacrificed on a banner of political vanity.

Niebuhr would dismiss the office-seeker who presumes to testify to God's will. While he thought it essential that religion play a vital role in public life, he believed its purpose was profoundly cautionary: religion could show Americans how to guard against the temptation to parade their righteousness. "Can the Church give a 'moral lead?'" he asked in 1959. He answered by suggesting how easily the church can misconceive its mission:

> If we seek to justify Christianity because it preserves democracy, or inspires a hatred for dictatorship, or makes a "free enterprise system" possible, or helps us to change our system into something better, or creates a "third force"—our utilitarian attitude debases

the Christian faith to the status of a mere instrument of the war-
ring creeds from which the world suffers.[6]

In seeking to sensitize the American mind to the reality of sin in the
world, Niebuhr was fond of William James's warning that "the trail
of the human serpent is over everything." He believed the rhetoric
of religious condemnation was nothing less than the sin of pride.
"Let us judge not that we be not judged," admonished Lincoln in
his second inaugural address, an admonition Niebuhr frequently
recalled. Today, alas, piety serves power; our leaders go to war convinced they are right with God.

Niebuhr's voice guided America through World War II and the
Cold War, but after the Vietnam War liberals ignored him, mistakenly equating his ideas with a reflexive anticommunism, while conservatives touted their own anticommunist credentials as badges
of moral clarity, successfully tarring liberals as the proponents of a
weak foreign policy born of moral relativism.

Today, in America's war on terror, Niebuhr's legacy is again invoked, but it continues to be misconstrued in the service of flawed
political ends. Some contemporary liberals look to Niebuhr for
counsel on ways to reclaim their lost reputation for muscular leadership in foreign policy. In 2006 the *New York Times Sunday Magazine* published "The Rehabilitation of the Cold War Liberal" by Peter Beinart, a former editor at the *New Republic*, accompanied by a
full-page photo of Niebuhr. Beinart argued that after 9/11 America
needed Niebuhr's wisdom because his example could show liberals
how to assert American power, battle evil to win the war on terror,
and recapture the glory days of liberalism.[7]

One wonders why our neo-Niebuhrians think Niebuhr would
have supported the invasion of Iraq, a preemptive war carried out
unilaterally and for reasons that require continual revision. "We are
not a sanctified nation," the theologian wrote in 1959,

> and we must not assume that all our actions are dictated by con-
> siderations of disinterested justice. If we fall into this error the
> natural resentments against our power on the part of the weaker

nations will be compounded with resentments against our pretensions to virtue. These resentments are indeed a part of the animus of anti-Americanism throughout the world.[8]

Niebuhr opposed the moral terms by which the Cold War came to be defined, and if he drew upon religion for political purposes, it was to foster skepticism and self-scrutiny, not to encourage arrogant self-assertion and rituals of righteousness.

Beinart claimed early Cold War liberals had demonstrated that capitalism could be coupled to domestic policy reform and international economic cooperation. But a market economy always lives uneasily with Christianity, and more recent attempts by neoconservatives to ground capitalism in Christian morality ignore Niebuhr's warnings against "our pretension to virtue." In *Wealth and Poverty* (1981), published at the start of the Reagan presidency, the writer George Gilder claimed that the public benefits of a commercial market are not the reward of avarice and self-interest but display the altruism of enterprise. Successful entrepreneurs work and invest to serve the needs of others. Similarly, the Catholic thinker Michael Novak was bold enough to deny the persuasive force of Max Weber's *The Protestant Ethic and the Spirit of Capitalism* by claiming that it was Catholicism that historically emphasized the creativity of entrepreneurship in service to God.[9]

Niebuhr, who died in 1971, would hardly be surprised to see how profits are equated with piety and religion is used to rationalize material acquisitiveness. He agreed with Nietzsche's view that "altruistic actions are only a species of egoistic actions" and that in self-justification individuals deny the motives for their own behavior.[10] With Augustine, Niebuhr understood that God implanted desire in human nature so that we never get as much as we want. Those who extol capitalism are romantics who exalt the self and its desires. But the Christian ideal of love, Niebuhr maintained, is heedless of the self and its craving for possession. Neoconservatives bear comparison to alchemists who conjure the identity of contraries, allowing humankind to indulge the pleasures of greed in the spirit of God—a transubstantiation Pascal called "treason." Americans may as well drive their SUVs through the eye of a needle.

If liberals have wanted Niebuhr to buttress their foreign policy credentials and neoconservatives need religion to support the market, radicals would just as soon forget religion and return to reason to attain the promise of freedom. Christopher Hitchens, once a Trotskyist and an ardent follower of Tom Paine, recently stated his position in the provocative and thoughtful *God Is Not Great*:

> Religion has run out of justifications. Thanks to the telescope and the microscope, it no longer offers an explanation of anything important. Where once it used to be able, by its total command of a world-view, to *prevent* the emergence of rivals, it can now only impede and retard—or try to turn back—the measurable advances that we have made. Sometimes, true, it will artfully concede them. But this is to offer itself the choice between irrelevance and obstruction, impotence or outright reaction, and, given this choice, it is programmed to select the worse of the two. Meanwhile, confronted with the undreamed-of vistas inside our own cortex, in the farthest reaches of the known universe, and in the proteins and acids which constitute our nature, religion offers annihilation in the name of god, or else the false promise that if we take a knife to our foreskin, or pray in the right direction, or ingest a piece of wafer, we shall be "saved." It is as if someone, offered a delicious and fragrant out-of-season fruit, matured in a painstakingly and lovingly designed hothouse, should throw away the flesh and the pulp and gnaw moodily on the pit.[11]

Hitchens has an answer to religion: "Above all, we are in need of a renewed Enlightenment." With the method of rational analysis bequeathed to us by the Enlightenment, we can study "literature and poetry" the way scientists approach "proteins and acids," and the "eternal ethical questions" dealt with in the humanities "can now easily depose the scrutiny of sacred texts that have been found to be corrupt and confected."

How easily? "Don't come to me with science," countered Nietzsche, for "it never creates values." Hitchens can praise what the telescope discovers, but, Nietzsche observed, "Since Copernicus man seems to have got himself on an inclined plane—now he is slipping faster and faster away from the centre into—what? into nothingness?" Humankind sees itself belittled, reduced to "nothing but a piece of bizarre conceit." Let us not delude ourselves, Nietzsche warned, by thinking that the philosophers of the Enlightenment were "emancipated from the theologians." Modern man thinks he attains knowledge, but everything he knows "does not merely fail to satisfy his desires but rather contradicts them and produces a sense of horror." Religion may have "run out of justifications," but the Enlightenment cannot justify itself.[12]

Hitchens's insistence that we are "in need of a renewed Enlightenment" perpetuates the notion that the eighteenth-century philosophes broke free of Christianity. For the philosophe, evil is simple ignorance, a deficiency, not a depravity. Enlightenment thinkers assumed as axiomatic humankind's continuity with nature. For Niebuhr this was no less an illusion than assuming the continuity of man with God. Niebuhr liked to cite Carl Becker's intellectual history of the mind of the Enlightenment, *The Heavenly City of the Eighteenth-Century Philosophers* (1932), to show that Enlightenment thinkers took assumptions that sustained religion and carried them over into science: reason would replace faith and nature God, but what remained was the claim to omniscience, a conviction that one could comprehend a revealed body of knowledge.

The religious mind may "gnaw moodily on the pit" of theology and metaphysical curiosity, as Hitchens asserts. But is that not because the Enlightenment has proved impotent to answer the deepest questions of the human condition? Where in the "cortex" can we find answers to the mystery of love, the sweetness and sorrows of memory, the burden of conscience, guilt, and moral judgment, the riddle of the self, the opaqueness of knowledge, the elusiveness of truth, the meaninglessness of suffering, the purpose of life, and, the final insult, its cessation in death? "Here today, gone tomorrow" is both an empirical statement and a glib maxim that invites our casual indifference. The Enlightenment increased humanity's power over nature but failed to provide an answer to Tolstoy's two questions: Why was I born? and For what should I live? Nor could it answer Niebuhr's overriding question: How is it that "an evil which does not exist in nature could have arisen in human history?"[13]

. . .

During the height of the Cold War, the eminent neoconservative intellectual Jeane Kirkpatrick, whom President Ronald Reagan appointed as US ambassador to the United Nations, grew understandably angry at the radical Left for its unrelenting criticisms of American foreign and domestic policies: "They always blame America first." Niebuhr could sympathize with her outrage, but he warned us against presuming that American policies are always right. Niebuhr cared less about Americans who always blame America than about those who always equate American history with divine Providence. The American character, so proud in its innocence, so vain in its arrogance, refuses to reflect on its own actions. Niebuhr was always willing to forgive his fellow Americans, but he asked them to be mindful of a question that goes to the heart of ethics and their moral responsibilities: How much evil might America do in attempting to do good?

1

"Seek with Groans":
The Making of a Theologian

Reinhold Niebuhr often denied that he was a theologian, calling himself instead an academic "circuit rider" who would bring the insights of Christianity to those who scorned it. Early in life he questioned whether he was a Christian, and colleagues and followers would speculate on whether he believed in or prayed to God. Such curiosities speak to Niebuhr's modesty more than to his identity. Niebuhr's lifelong doubts about his religious vocation link him to Blaise Pascal, the seventeenth-century French Catholic philosopher who would "seek with groans," searching for truth and God while lamenting that he could find neither through reason.[1]

Niebuhr believed with other thinkers that to be skeptical about God is not only a matter of honesty but a necessity for a good Christian. Even Sidney Hook, the atheist who sided with the philosopher of pragmatism John Dewey against Niebuhr, could not help but acknowledge that he was in the presence of a mind as humble as it was profound. "There must be something extremely paradoxical in the thought of Reinhold Niebuhr," wrote Hook, "to make so many who are so far apart in their own allegiances feel so akin to him."[2]

THE 1920S AND THE CRISIS OF LIBERAL CHRISTIANITY

Reinhold Niebuhr was born in Wright City, Missouri, in 1892, the son of a German immigrant father who became a rural Protestant minister. The father, Gustav, was a scholarly evangelical who showed little interest in the Social Gospel reform movement roiling American Protestantism during the Progressive era. Reinhold studied at his father's alma mater, Eden Theological Seminary, near Saint Louis, where he worked to overcome the limitations of his German background and to master English. By the time he entered Yale Divinity School in 1913, he was convinced that religion must be grounded in human needs and experience, not in supernatural revelation. With the philosopher William James, he understood the truth of religion to lie within the human capacity to experience it. He also agreed with Pascal's dictum that genuine religion is always a struggle between belief and unbelief, and this capacity to doubt the illusions of certainty would become central to Niebuhr's religious vocation and to his political convictions as well.[3]

Niebuhr first grappled with politics at the outbreak of World War I. In a 1915 student essay, "The Paradox of Patriotism," he echoed James's 1906 essay "The Moral Equivalent of War" in arguing that despite its undoubted brutality war afforded the individual opportunities to show courage and selflessness. With America's entry into the war in 1917, the son of the German immigrant even participated in the Wilson administration's campaign against "disloyalty," succumbing to the president's fervent call to prosecute "a war to end all wars." But the political compromises of the Paris Peace Conference caused Niebuhr to become disillusioned with the promises of Wilsonian liberalism, and in the early 1920s, while many American intellectuals were bidding farewell to politics, he grew ever more engaged in it.

After the injustices of World War I and the cynicism of the peace settlement, the world looked different. Faith in the unseen was devastated by what was all too apparent: the slaughter and pestilence of trench warfare, civilian starvation, and the betrayal of Wilson's pledge to "make the world safe for democracy." History no longer seemed to dramatize a story of progress and perfectibility; it appeared cruel and vindictive. Rejecting the high hopes of the politicians of the prewar period and the then-prevailing liberal Protestantism of its clerics and academics, Niebuhr set out to develop a new approach to Christianity for a modern world that could no longer believe in historical progress or rational order, a religion fit for an age of anxiety, for man's despairing predicament in a meaningless world.

The young Niebuhr was invited to serve as pastor of Bethel Evangelical Church in Detroit, and it was here that he discovered the harshness of industrial society, the toil of the laboring classes and the complacency of the propertied. When Bruce Barton, the advertising agency pioneer, wrote a best seller, *The Man Nobody Knows* (1925), that described Jesus as the first successful publicist and a role model for modern business executives, Niebuhr responded with a blistering review in the *Christian Century*, denouncing the industrialists' professions of piety and lamenting the culture of consumption that was overwhelming middle-class America. It was but one in a growing number of articles Niebuhr would write challenging the nation's political apathy and moral indifference to social wrongs.

A charismatic speaker with a growing reputation, Niebuhr was much in demand. He chafed at his church duties and welcomed invitations from across the country to preach on religion and society. He upset members of his congregation by inviting union leaders to speak from the pulpit and wrote articles attacking the benevolence of Detroit's own Henry Ford. In 1928, after thirteen years at Bethel, he accepted a teaching position at Union Theological Seminary, a center for liberal Christianity in New York City.

Mention the name Reinhold Niebuhr today and what comes to mind is a Cold War liberal who denounced the menace of communism. Niebuhr did indeed do that in the 1940s and 1950s, but decades earlier, before the rise of Hitler and Stalin, the theologian was at war with America itself. It was a war he would lose, as would fascists, communists, and anyone else who dared challenge America's political culture of striving and success. "To be rich is glorious!"

China's Deng Xiaoping once declared. Niebuhr would hardly be surprised by the pronouncement of the Communist Party leader. A century earlier, in *Democracy in America*, the French visitor Alexis de Tocqueville had described how commerce overcomes culture. Tocqueville did not need the term "consumer capitalism" to give an account of Americans kept in a constant state of agitation by the pursuit of material happiness and its "petty pleasures." The "equality and precariousness of their social condition," he wrote, had made Americans into strivers consumed by "a restless and insatiable vanity" and a "taste for physical comfort."[4]

By the mid-1920s America was further confirming Tocqueville's impressions. F. Scott Fitzgerald's *The Great Gatsby* appeared in 1925, and what troubled Niebuhr the theologian was precisely what haunted Fitzgerald the novelist: the surrender and absorption of the self into the whirlwind of society. Niebuhr always insisted that the focus of theology should be on the self, which can be virtuous in the presence of God's grace. But in the 1920s America went on what Fitzgerald called "the greatest, the gaudiest spree in history."[5]

After World War I the old moral obligations and civic duties began to crumble, and a pleasure-seeking public lost itself in the pursuit of excitement and glamour. Instead of memorializing the noble deeds of great leaders, an emerging mass media—advertisers, popular magazines, the movies, and radio—held out an endless supply of entertainment for the common man, who was urged to identify with wealth and celebrity. Writers and intellectuals during the Jazz Age sensed the nation's break with its past, and their work reflected the discontinuity with what had gone before them. In his confessional essay "The Crack-Up" (1936), Fitzgerald recalled the change in his feelings for New York City, the empty merriment that gave way to boredom and loneliness, and how he had allowed his identity to fall under the influence of others until he discovered there "was no 'I' any more. . . . It was strange to have no self—to be like a little boy left alone in a big house, who knew now he could do anything he wanted to do, but found there was nothing he wanted to do."[6]

Niebuhr could have reminded Fitzgerald of what the Calvinists had warned the colonists of early New England: the Christian will lose his soul if he allows the sovereignty of God to be absorbed into the norms of society. In the 1920s Niebuhr faced just this condition: his country regarded prosperity as the measure of morality. It was as though the Christian dualism of God and Mammon had found its higher synthesis on Wall Street.

"Love of possessions," wrote Niebuhr, "is a distraction which makes love and obedience to God impossible." For Niebuhr Americans could never overcome the love of possessions because sin is ineradicable: the flesh and the spirit are in a permanent state of war. The theologian argued that the dualisms of religion—good and evil, spirit and matter, freedom and fate—cannot be reconciled because each is part of our humanity and each requires the other to convey the meaning of Christianity. "The test of a first-rate intelligence," observed Fitzgerald, "is the ability to hold two opposed ideas in the mind at the same time, and still retain the ability to function"—a perfect description of Niebuhr's intellect.[7]

THE PROBLEM OF PRIDE

The realm of "mystery" in religion lies, Simone Weil observed, "at the intersection of creation and its Creator."[8] In his role as a teacher Reinhold Niebuhr did not propose to solve the mystery, but he would go to that intersection, the juncture where man can hope to feel God's presence while acknowledging God's absence.

Niebuhr's theology is a study in both the limitations of knowledge and the necessity of faith. Man is estranged, God is in exile, and the nineteenth-century attempt to find God in history is a chimera. History is tragic because man is finite. The Supreme Being can do little to elevate man above his human condition. Only man can save himself as he sees that "the abyss of meaninglessness yawns on the brink of all his mighty spiritual endeavors."[9]

For Niebuhr, religion begins not with reason and thinking but with the self and its anxieties. Anxiety is "the inevitable spiritual state of man" and "the internal precondition of sin":

Man, being both free and bound, both limited and limitless, is anxious. Anxiety is the inevitable concomitant of the paradox of freedom and finiteness in which man is involved.

Against social reformers and liberal Christians, Niebuhr argued
that reason cannot be expected to overcome human weakness.
What stands in the way is not ignorance but sin. Sin is the pretension to knowledge and the aspiration to moral achievement that
betrays a will to power. Man is always "tempted to deny the limited
character of his knowledge and the finiteness of his perspectives."[10]

From Aristotle and Augustine to Rousseau and Hume, the self
has always been problematic; it is the battleground of reason and
passion left bloody with unsatisfied cravings. In American intellectual history, however, once one gets beyond Jonathan Edwards and
other Calvinist explorers of the inner life, the self becomes less a
riddle and more a resource. Consider terms common to the American experience: self-government, self-interest, self-determination,
self-reliance, self-esteem, self-consciousness. Such expressions assume that freedom depends on the strengths of the self. These are
the very tendencies Niebuhr identified with sin.[11]

Many of Niebuhr's contemporaries, especially liberals and pragmatists, could only wonder what the theologian was getting at.
There is, they insisted, no primordial self trapped within its own
tendencies and temptations; there is only a "social" or "looking-
glass" self, shaped by the mind's interactions with others and by
the social forces that impinge upon it. Thought's reflections have no
reference beyond the contexts of society. Some pragmatists almost
found a moral equivalent to religion in the new discipline of sociology, whose insights appeared to absolve and redeem the troubled
conscience by showing how it was produced by the processes of society. Niebuhr, however, was convinced that the "sociological turn"
in modern thought led to moral complacency. Indeed, if the self, the
seed of selfishness, has no independent existence, then sin disappears as well, as it did for John Dewey, Niebuhr's great antagonist.[12]
In contemporary European thought the self disappears almost entirely. It is a "social construction" or a "linguistic trope," a projec-

tion of political ideology or a convention of language waiting to be deconstructed. By identifying anxiety in the self as the seed of sin, Niebuhr radically departs from these currents of thought.

In his first systematic treatise in theology, *An Interpretation of Christian Ethics* (1935), Niebuhr observed that the self's absorption into society was a characteristic of the Social Gospel movement. During the Progressive era the theologian Walter Rauschenbusch argued that Christians could reorganize humanity's collective life according to the will of God by better understanding how individual behavior is shaped by social institutions. Arthur Schlesinger Jr. noted that Rauschenbusch himself was no naïve social reformer. But many of his followers did believe life could be freed of struggle and sin once reform joined with religion and science to transform society and alter the progress of history. The Social Gospel proposed to apply love rather than power to politics.[13]

Niebuhr broke profoundly with these tendencies. In the nineteenth century it was common to regard the events of history as demonstrations of the advance of reason and social progress. Philosophers like Hegel absorbed religion into history and nature, promising thereby to reveal the ways of God to man. For Hegel, God was immanent in history, no longer a transcendent judge. For the naturalist Charles Darwin, God was inherent in the processes of the biological world. Evolving, unfolding, progressing, God was no supreme being but rather a "becoming," responsive to the acts of man and the mutations of the species. The Hegelian and Darwinian notion that Spirit dwells in human and natural history was a major influence on Christian doctrine in the nineteenth century; it gave a new meaning to the old idea of faith as the evidence of things unseen.

Niebuhr asserted that this sort of rationalized religion had succeeded only too well in accommodating itself to civilization and its contentments:

> The whole modern secular liberal culture, to which liberal Christianity is unduly bound, is really a devitalized and secularized religion in which the presuppositions of a Christian tradition have

been rationalized and read into the processes of history and nature, supposedly discovered by objective science. The original tension of Christian morality is thereby destroyed; for the transcendent ideals of Christian morality have become immanent possibilities in the historic process. Democracy, mutual cooperation, the League of Nations, international trade reciprocity, and other similar conceptions are regarded as the ultimate ideals of the human spirit. None of them are without some degree of absolute validity, but modern culture never discovered to what degree they had emerged out of the peculiar conditions and necessities of a commercial civilization and were intimately related to the interests of the classes which have profited most by the expansion of commerce and industry in recent decades. The transcendent impossibilities of the Christian ethic of love became, in modern culture, the immanent and imminent possibilities of an historical process; and the moral complacence of a generation is thereby supported rather than challenged.[14]

Niebuhr's criticisms of liberal religion bear traces of Marx and Nietzsche, for whom religion perpetuates a "false consciousness." Nietzsche held that by postulating God, "a stupendous concept" that is "merely a mistake of man's," Christianity humbled humankind, leaving it too weak to experience its own alienation. Marx expected the proletariat to banish Christianity, which, by appearing to respond to "the sigh of the oppressed creature," masks the selfishness of the propertied.[15]

Niebuhr argued that liberal religion and liberalism obscure the sources of selfishness they claim to rectify. He wanted to save Christianity from its too-easy identification with secular reform, which misunderstands the causes of the world's conflicts and the self's temptations.

In the 1920s Niebuhr still retained some of the idealistic optimism of the Social Gospel. He joined the pacifist Fellowship of Reconciliation, wrote for *World Tomorrow* and *Christian Century*, and published his first book, *Does Civilization Need Religion?* (1927). But during the Depression years of the 1930s, with their grim breadlines and brutal labor strikes, Niebuhr grew impatient with those who professed to believe that moral conduct, scientific intelligence, and religious goodwill could achieve the Kingdom of God. Liberal Protestantism, he now complained, was afflicted by "blindness toward the darker depths of life. The 'sin' of Christian orthodoxy was translated into the imperfections of ignorance, which an adequate pedagogy would soon overcome."[16]

Niebuhr protested that the real "sin" was the false assumption of the liberal reformer that his own mind could comprehend itself and the world, and that he was able to subdue the "evil impulses" that were "defying and mocking his conscious control and his rational moral pretensions." It was a mistake to credit the reformer's optimistic conviction "that all the forces which determine each moral and social situation were fully known and completely understood, and that the forces of reason had successfully chained all demonic powers." Religious exponents of the Social Gospel, as well as secular sociologists and pragmatists, foolishly persuaded themselves that they had knowledge of the causes and conditions that determine human behavior, and that they could apply this knowledge to change the world. Confident that they had achieved an unprecedented level of self-awareness and self-control, the reformers were ready to flick away older views of religion like ashes from a cigarette. In Niebuhr's estimation, the modern mind mistook as depths of wisdom what were really the deceits of pride.[17]

For centuries the idea of pride has tied the threads of intellectual history in knots. Building self-esteem is an essential goal of our own time, as teachers urge students to take pride in themselves and their accomplishments in school. Pride, however, worries religious thinkers more than secular ones. We read in the Bible that God expelled Adam and Eve from Paradise because they disobeyed his command not to eat fruit from the tree that gives knowledge of good and evil. Augustine believed pride interfered with the purification that draws man nearer to God. At the dawn of modern liberalism, the political philosopher Thomas Hobbes believed Leviathan would have to rule over the "children of pride" who chose sovereignty over submission.

But if pride prompts the disobedience that leads to knowledge and freedom, why does Niebuhr condemn it? To the theologian pride has a number of meanings, none of them edifying. It can signify self-love of the kind that seeks social approval or a lust for power and possessions. It can incite a jingoistic nationalism, stir feelings of racial superiority, keep the mind from admitting its mistakes, or cause professors and clergymen to lord it over the unenlightened and unblessed. In Christianity it is the ultimate warning: Pride goeth before the Fall. "Any careful analysis of life," wrote Niebuhr, "reveals that a goodly portion of the misery which we bring upon each other in our social intercourse is due to pride."[18]

For Niebuhr pride is a sin in the heart of humanity. By contrast, the transcendental poet Ralph Waldo Emerson, whom Nietzsche admired, opposed whatever hindered the self and smothered the "Over-Soul." Like Nietzsche, Emerson believed self-abnegation leads to self-alienation. For the philosopher and the poet sin was a false idea invented by punitive religions. Both exalted "self-reliance" in order to know thyself and be thyself, and thus to be free from bondage to others. Not so Niebuhr, for whom the anxious self is in bondage to itself, and profoundly aware of the omnipresence of sin.

REVISING JESUS

Niebuhr reminds us that sin is a spiritual act, freely taken in the interests of the self and in rebellion against God. It is neither a temptation of the devil nor a compulsion arising from some psychological repression. Neither is it entirely a surrender to either nature or human finiteness at the expense of spirit and in defiance of God. In his essay "The Ethic of Jesus," Niebuhr points out that Jesus never "condemns natural impulse as inherently bad."[19] But here begins a problem. Jesus's ethic is not exclusively of this world or the next; it should neither be confused with the "ascetic ethic of world-denying religions nor with the prudential morality of naturalism, designed to guide good people to success and happiness in this world." Rather, Jesus's ethic is based on the "love ideal," which proceeds logically from prophetic religion, in which God, as creator and judge of the world, is both the unity which is the ground of existence and the ultimate unity, the good which is, to use Plato's phrase, on the other side of existence. In as far as the world exists at all it is good; for existence is possible only when chaos is overcome by unity and order. But the unity of the world is threatened by chaos, and its meaningfulness is always under the peril of meaninglessness.[20]

Is the ethic of Jesus sufficient for mankind? It is noteworthy that Niebuhr's own ethical teaching does not rely on it. Indeed, the theologian appeared at times compelled to remind the Savior not to forget that there is sin in the world. Paraphrasing Jesus, Niebuhr writes, "Since God permits the sun to shine upon the evil and the good and sends rain upon the just and unjust, we are to love our enemies." Jesus's command is just, but Niebuhr notes that Jesus proposes "emulation of the character of God" as "the only motive of forgiving enemies." "Nothing is said about the possibility of transmuting their enmity to friendship through the practice of forgiveness"; nor does Jesus have anything to say about resolving rivalries that lead to war, punishing criminals, or fighting for one's own survival. By loving one's enemies Jesus invokes the peace of God, but Niebuhr cautions against confusing this with the peace of the world, which, although conditional, is critical if there is to be justice:

> With Augustine we must realize that the peace of the world is gained by strife. That does not justify us either in rejecting such a tentative peace or in accepting it as final. The peace of the city of God can use and transmute the lesser and insecure peace of the city of the world; but that can be done only if the peace of the world is not confused with the ultimate peace of God.[21]

Niebuhr further diminishes the love ideal by suggesting in the politest terms that Jesus who died on the cross cannot be expected to offer useful instruction to humankind on how to live. What is one to make of Jesus's counsel against caring for one's physical needs?

Jesus firmly instructs those who are obedient to God that they must not calculate the consequences of this world:

Take no thought for your life, what ye shall eat, or what ye shall drink; nor yet for your body, what ye shall put on. Is not the life more than meat and the body more than raiment? Behold the fowls of the air; for they sow not, neither do they reap, nor gather into barns; yet your heavenly Father feedeth them.[22]

"Lay up not for yourselves treasures upon earth," he admonishes, "for where your treasure is, there will your heart be also." Rather, "Go and sell what thou hast, and give to the poor."[23]

Not afraid to contradict Jesus, Niebuhr notes that a concern for the physical basis of life cannot be left to a "naïve faith in God's providential care." The self has to be able to take care of itself to survive and succeed, and "the most natural expansion of the self is the expansion through possessions." "The very basis of self-love," he explains, "is the natural will to survive," which leads to the "immediate temptation to assert the self against the neighbor," which leads to all the aggression and conflict in the world. And yet, like other modern thinkers (Tocqueville, Nietzsche, Weber), Niebuhr knew modern society would never heed Jesus's counsel. Instead it would undertake its own "transvaluation" of Christian values to uphold success "at the price of sacrifice, abnegation, and loss."

Did not Jesus teach the ultimate contradiction? "He that findeth his life shall lose it; and he that loseth his life for my sake, shall find it." Niebuhr is untroubled by the irony:

This paradox merely calls attention to the fact that egoism is self-defeating, while self-sacrifice actually leads to a higher form of self-realization. Thus self-love is never justified, but self-realization is allowed as the unintended but inevitable consequences of unselfish action.[24]

Niebuhr warns, however, that unselfish actions still may be a conceit if they cause persons to believe they are above a common humanity where all are equal in God's eyes. This is "the spiritual pride and self-righteousness which fails to detect the alloy of sin" in all human action.[25]

Niebuhr loved paradox, and he loved to reveal paradox in politics and religion, especially when it offered a promise of redemption. The paradox of Jesus's teaching is its injunction to live in a state of suspended disbelief, a condition as mind-denying as the Hegelian-Marxist dialectic. The self is told to find life by losing it, which is not unlike the proletarian who is told to create democracy by dictatorship and peace by revolution. The dialectic, Niebuhr's contemporary Max Eastman once observed, "is like a mental disease; you don't know what it is until you get it, and then you don't know because you've got it."[26] Niebuhr got it both ways. When Jesus asks sinners to be saints he absentmindedly forgets humankind's fallen nature. Were humanity to follow his ethic it would deprive the Savior of the sins of the world that make his sacrifice necessary. Jesus's ethic, like the Marxian dialectic, is incapable of fulfillment—at least in this world.

Niebuhr's effort to remind Jesus about sin was his way of teaching liberal Protestants lessons about life. In America, religious progressives wanted to follow sweet Jesus. With a lamblike innocence of sin in a world without evil, they eagerly embraced scientific knowledge and rational explanation and left theology back in the Middle Ages. In the first part of the twentieth century, all academic disciplines, including the liberal arts, looked for validation from science and the material measurement of evidence. Niebuhr, more interested in the quest for meaning than the rules of methodology, firmly believed religion has a right to truths independent of, and perhaps contrary to, the conclusions of science. One of those truths is the splendor of sin.

Niebuhr recounted sin's many manifestations: it is man's pride in looking to power to secure himself against life's contingencies and vicissitudes; finite man's presumption of knowing God's will and what is virtuous; the weakness of the flesh in succumbing to sensual pleasures; the rationalizing self that regards its own egoistic acts as though they are disinterested. And, finally, sin manifests itself as an inordinate self-love that has no place for God, which gives way to an existential despair that was anticipated by Augustine and apprehended by Kierkegaard: "This is the meaning of Kierkegaard's assertion that sin posits itself."[27]

Yet Niebuhr also saw the affirmative aspect of sin, which can prompt a sense of guilt that stimulates self-awareness. "The sense of sin is a sense of finiteness before the infinite, a feeling in which the metaphysical emphasis imperils the ethical connotation" when one comes face to face with the problem of evil and wrestles with the paradox of fate and freedom. Ethics demands we do good; metaphysics declares we are born to evil. Wrestling with original sin, grace, and predestination. Niebuhr summed up man's predicament: "He can see what he cannot reach."[28]

THE PARADOX OF LOVE

In pondering the plight of theology in the modern world, Niebuhr avoided drawing upon the two foundations of old world Catholic philosophy. The first was Aquinas's idea of "natural law," which commands us to follow our own nature to obey the law that inclines us to the good. We are to "do good and avoid evil" because all living things move under the impulses of desire and aversion. The second was Pascal's conviction that life's central question concerns death and immortality and that, in the face of certain annihilation, believing in God is a wager worth making.

Neither position seemed convincing to Niebuhr. To be told that we are moved by the drives of desire and aversion could very well be a definition of sin, in which our natural human egoism aims at its self-satisfaction. Likewise, Pascal's fear of death and desire for immortality offers as a solution what is really the problem. A religious thinker who would explain the desire for God in terms compatible with a naturalistic ethics

> will always see the total situation in which he is involved only from
> a limited perspective; he will never be able to divorce his reason
> from its organic relation with the natural impulse of survival with

which nature has endowed him; and he will never be able to escape the sin of accentuating his natural will-to-live into an impe-
rial will-to-power by the very protest which his yearning for the
eternal tempts him to make against his finiteness.[29]

Enlightenment thinkers criticized Pascal, the "sublime misan-
thrope" in Voltaire's estimate, for telling humanity how horrifying
life is; Pascal's religious defenders responded that he was only trying to make us aware that we conceal ourselves from ourselves in
order to think better of ourselves. Niebuhr's point was that the fear
of death instills anxiety in the finite man. Most attempt to overcome anxiety through the acquisition of power and possessions.
Pascal, however, was so possessed by the prospect of death that he
couldn't wait to flee the world and win his wager.

Had Catholic theology concentrated on the mystery of faith,
Niebuhr would have raised no objection. With Aquinas, however,
it was not spiritual longing but logical reasoning that promised
to deliver humankind from its existential predicament. For the
Thomist, sin is more than an offense against God: It is contrary to
reason. Niebuhr recognized the importance of reason in inquiry.
In science, reason demands proof, evidence, and verification; in
philosophy, consistency, coherence, and clarity. But Niebuhr asked
how sin could be contrary to reason when sin is the very expression
of humankind's finite nature.

Niebuhr liked to invoke Pascal against Aquinas and other Catholic thinkers, reminding them that man—a finite creature who seeks
the infinite—has a dual nature, one both free and determined, acting and acted upon, a self tempted to do evil while struggling to
fulfill the law of love. A free spirit and creature of nature is a living
contradiction, noted Niebuhr, and this dilemma led

Pascal to elaborate his Christian existentialism in opposition to the
Cartesian rationalism and Jesuit Thomism of his day. Pascal delved
"in my mysteries without which man remains a mystery to himself"; and that phrase may be a good introduction to the consider-

ation of the relation of supernatural affirmations of the Christian faith to the antinomies, contradictions, and mysteries of human existence.[30]

In contrast to Pascal, Aquinas postulated that nothing happens without a reason. Everything must have a prior cause until we reach an uncaused cause or first cause, "and this we call God." But in trying to infer God's existence through logic, Aquinas denied God freedom and even a little fun as well, since he could not change his mind or his ways. The historian Henry Adams caught the dilemma in a single sentence: "St. Thomas did not allow the Deity the right to contradict Himself, which is one of man's chief pleasures."[31]

Niebuhr sought out intellectual forebears and companions who would buttress his convictions. Besides Pascal, he found in the nineteenth-century Danish theologian Søren Kierkegaard a kindred spirit who explored the dual nature and inner contradictions of man as both free spirit and contingent object. Niebuhr appreciated Kierkegaard's sense of history as a haunting drama of human striving and divine will, but he had reservations about the Dane's belief in his own "passionate subjectivity" as the sole test of truth. Kierkegaard's idea of love was also troubling in that it resembled Kant's idea of duty: it was so abstract and universal as to be separate from human experience. "There is no grace, no freedom, no release in it. It is full of the sweat of a plodding righteousness, and it hides the fact of the self-continued finiteness."[32]

Some critics compared Niebuhr to his contemporary, the Swiss theologian Karl Barth, who also scorned liberal Protestantism's efforts to accommodate religion to reason. Like Niebuhr, Barth asserted the sovereignty of God and the universality of sin. But the doctrines he propounded put God so far beyond human comprehension that theology would have had to issue a missing persons alert to find him. Barth's God offered little comfort or wisdom to the human seeker, who had to sit back and wait for his revelation. "This is a religion," Niebuhr concluded, paraphrasing a Catholic critic, "which is fashioned for the catacombs and has little relation to the task of transfiguring the natural stuff of politics by the grace and wisdom of the gospel."[33]

· · ·

In his two-volume *The Nature and Destiny of Man* (1941, 1943), Niebuhr made his most sustained inquiry into the nature and purpose of the human self, offering a sweeping survey of its treatment in the history of Western philosophy and theology. The book, derived from the Gifford Lectures Niebuhr delivered at the University of Edinburgh beginning in 1939, evaluated classical, medieval, and modern views of human nature and offered a Christian interpretation of the meaning of human history.

Niebuhr began by contrasting classical philosophy to Christianity. The ancients understood man as a dualism of mind and body, a repository of virtue and vice locked in eternal combat. Christianity added a prophetic and paradoxical dimension to the reasoning self—expanding finite man's capacity for self-transcending freedom. However, while man is made in God's image and "the law of his nature is love," man is yet again a sinner, and evil is at "the very centre of the human personality—in the will." "Sin is occasioned," observed Niebuhr, "precisely by the fact that man refused to admit his 'creatureliness' and to acknowledge himself as merely a member of a total unity of life. He pretends to be more than he is." This pretense drives the self into egocentrism and desecrates the miracle of love as "man seeks to make himself the centre and source of his own life. His sin is therefore spiritual and not carnal, though the infection of rebellion spreads from the spirit to the body and disturbs its harmonies also."[34]

Many modern thinkers—in particular, Nietzsche, Freud, and Weber—took up the theme of the divided and estranged self, but Niebuhr noted that existential ideas are largely subordinate to science and naturalism in modern thought. Modern rationalism plays down individuality, the flower of the Renaissance, and repudiates sin, the shadow of the Reformation. Thus modern man has an essentially easy conscience; and nothing gives the diverse and discordant notes of modern culture so much harmony as the unanimous opposition of modern man to the Christian conception of the sinfulness of man.

Whether he is conceived as rational and intelligent or as natural and good, "it is only necessary for man either to rise from the chaos of nature to the harmony of mind or to descend from the chaos of spirit to the harmony of nature to be saved."[35]

If mind or nature will not save us, where should we turn? Although a Protestant steeped in the teachings of Luther and Calvin, Niebuhr advised against returning to the Reformation. Niebuhr admired Martin Luther for synthesizing God's grace with his forgiveness and love. Yet the scenario spelled submission: "The soul is the 'poor little harlot' who brings nothing to the spiritual marriage but a 'sackfull of sins' and her 'rich bridegroom Christ' brings all the goodness." That Christ brings all the goods and does all the work of salvation was too much for Niebuhr, who questioned Luther's refutation of free will and his account of man's utter depravity without God's saving grace. Niebuhr believed the Lutheran Reformation was too "defeatist" and left humanity unable to sustain a robust social ethics to show men how to fulfill their obligations to one another.[36]

Protestantism was made even more fatalistic by John Calvin, who preached justification by faith and rejected justification by works. Whether in Luther or in Calvin, the doctrine of justification by "faith alone" meant "man's acceptance of grace by faith, rather than grace itself, becomes determinative." "This error," observed Niebuhr, "betrayed Luther into a rejection of whatever goodness may be realized outside the Christian life." In American history, Jonathan Edwards preached in vain to colonials who expected their works to reward them in this life, while the righteousness conferred by faith alone led to the doctrine of antinomianism and Anne Hutchinson, who would lecture the magistrates of the Massachusetts Bay Colony that she would do whatever she wanted, for whatever she did was predestined by God's will. The Reformation's concept of grace, Niebuhr advised, promoted pessimism and passivity and gave inadequate sanction for moral action.[37]

Did Catholicism have a better solution? Its conception of grace intrigued Niebuhr but left him dissatisfied. Aquinas acknowledged that God's grace allows man to do good and avoid sin, and he made the point that the movement of our will "is not the cause of grace but the result of it. The whole operation is therefore due to grace." But what activates the will? Since "the first movement of will or any appetitive power is love," human beings are compelled by an innate impulse of the will toward the good. Here is the point at which the Catholic appeals to natural law and where the scholastic doctor's answer seems ambiguous. "But is Aquinas saying quite so little as that we desire the desirable or that men seek what they seek?" asks F. C. Copleston, the Jesuit historian of philosophy.[38]

Catholic scholars as learned as Copleston and as brilliant as Etienne Gilson have used up much paper and ink explicating the fine points of Thomism. But in Niebuhr's judgment, Saint Thomas fatally deprived religion of anxiety, the one attribute that can sustain it. Luther at least understood that the power of reason is tainted with pride, but Aquinas was confident that "the redeemed man actually stands beyond the sin of history in fact as well as in principle." The optimism of the Catholic view brings down the curtain on the drama of the troubled soul: God's grace and man's reason can overcome sin because sin is "the privation of an original perfection, rather than . . . a positive corruption." Niebuhr argued that in Aquinas's "formulation the conformity of the human to the divine will is well nigh absolute, and the only sin which remains is occasioned by vagrant impulses below the level of the will." These impulses—the venial sins—are "due to a lack of perfect submission of the will to God." Catholicism is a formulation not so much for freedom as surrender.[39]

Niebuhr's own formulation imputed to the character of God what God himself never deigned to acknowledge. In Niebuhr's account, God has an eternal identity crisis, for the Creator does not know who he is, whether sovereign and rational or contradictory and incoherent, whether the verdict of judgment and punishment or the voice of mercy and forgiveness. Niebuhr believed Aquinas was mistaken to think that "it is possible for a will centered in an individual ego to be brought into essential conformity with the will and power which governs all things." Instead the American theologian argued that it is precisely because of the contradictory nature of a deity thought to be all powerful that "the self is free to defy God" in order to assert the dignity of man and rise above his misery.[40]

Where does this leave a god who claims supreme sovereignty over all the things of his creation? "The Christian's chief and only comfort in every adversity," wrote Martin Luther, "lies in knowing that God does not lie, but brings all things to pass immutably, and that His will cannot be resisted, altered or impeded." Niebuhr would probably answer that Christians are already too satisfied that they are following God and doing the right thing. What is necessary instead is the freedom of the will, without which morality is impossible and love inconceivable.[41]

The miracle of love has been characterized as a spiritually expansive act of giving oneself to another. For Niebuhr love is the "pull" of the self out of the egoistic calculations of interest and pleasure, the awareness of the "possible impossibility" of self-realization through self-sacrifice. Niebuhr reminds us that no authority can order the self to love that which is right and good. "To command love is a paradox; for love cannot be commanded or demanded. To love God with all our hearts and all our souls and all our minds means that every cleavage in human existence is overcome."[42]

The Thomist thinks love is a natural impulse, a desire to seek the good as reason leads the will to overcome turbulent passions. Natural man is "under the obligation to emulate the love of God, to forgive as God forgives, to love his enemies as God loves them."[43] But Niebuhr insists that while the finite self always strains to achieve the transcendent it always backslides into sin.

It is amazing that Niebuhr extracted a compelling moral and political philosophy from Christianity yet made no argument for the existence of God, whose name is unmentioned in the titles of his many books. Niebuhr's major biographer, Richard Fox, claims the theologian relied on the philosopher William James for assurance that one could believe in God without knowing him:

> Having decided what type of God he needed, Niebuhr proceeded to invoke William James's pragmatism to justify the act of belief itself. James's "will to believe," even in the absence of strict verification, was rooted in the conviction that the act of knowing was not an "outward look." Truth was not something to be possessed once and for all, not a final apprehension of reality, but something to be worked toward, approximated, in action.[44]

Perhaps so, but we need to remind ourselves that pragmatism is a philosophy that postpones the search for truth, making truth an emotional construction more than a philosophical conviction. "Truth happens to an idea," James declared. "It *becomes true*, it is *made* true by events."

Can we make God become true? Niebuhr admired James's book *The Varieties of Religious Experience* (1902) and praised its chapter on saintliness. Yet he declared that James's "analysis of religious life is defective" because it showed no concern for "the meaning of human history." James was interested in religion's psychological effects more than its moral guidance for politics and social action. Niebuhr wisely never troubled himself over God's existence. All that James could offer Niebuhr was the comfort of belief, not the reliability of knowledge. As George Santayana said of James, "He did not really believe; he merely believed in the right of believing that you might be right if you believed."[45]

THE TEASE OF THEOLOGY

H. L. Mencken argued that Christianity "goes to pieces with the problem of evil" and followed his mentor Nietzsche in trying to laugh good and evil out of the world. But for religious thinkers the problem is always: How does evil get into the world? If God is omnipotent and his creation is good, whence evil? The question that consumed Augustine hasn't disappeared because postmodernity claims to have banished the "spooks" of religion and metaphysics. In Archibald MacLeish's play *J.B.* man can only utter what he fails to understand:

> I heard it in a yellow wood.
> If God is God He is not good.
> If God is good He is not God.[46]

MacLeish's 1959 play is a riff on the book of Job, which scholars tell us dates from the fifth to seventh centuries BC. How to understand the reasons for pain and suffering and the monstrous injustices and disasters inflicted on the good and innocent: They can scarcely be explained by a Christian theory of reward and punishment. The solution to "the problem of Job" proposed by the philosopher Josiah Royce—that God suffers along with mankind—made Santayana laugh at the thought of God as a masochist. Job's own solution puts the blame on lowly mortals. What appears evil is really good were we but wise enough to see it.

Congregations typically expect their pastors to explain God's mysterious ways. Niebuhr recalled one incident that stayed with him:

> I remember when I was a young parson, two Sunday school girls were playing under the window of my study. One said, "Let's not make too much noise; we will disturb Mr. Niebuhr." And the other little girl said, "Who is Mr. Niebuhr?" The first child answered, "Don't you know? He is the pastor to this church. He knows all about God."

The children did not understand that biblical faith conveys the concealment of God as well as the disclosure of his presence. For Christians, as Charles C. Brown has written of the anecdote, "the revelation through Christ does not completely dissolve mystery. Clergy and theologians, he [Niebuhr] added, do well not to pretend to knowing more about God than anybody can know."[47]

At the very beginning of the *Summa Theologica*, Thomas Aquinas advises, "We cannot know what God is, but rather only what He is not," and he suggests that on such matters ignorance may be the better part of knowledge: "This is the extreme of human knowledge of God: To know that we do not know God." Aquinas seeks to explain the ways of God, convinced that he exists, that he is one, and that he is good. "But it is most apparent," writes Etienne Gilson,

> that there is knowledge of the divine nature infinitely beyond the grasp of the human understanding. This is a point which it is important to establish in order to silence the unbelievers who consider false all statements about God which our reason is unable to make.[48]

According to Niebuhr it is sin that comes between man and God, the corruption of the will plays havoc with knowledge, and consequently the attempt to know God or confer meaning upon him is a mark of pride. The essence of the Christian religion is the dialectic between grace and pride. Whether Niebuhr offers a resolution or only a suspension to the riddles of faith is itself a riddle. Leszek Kolakowski has written that attempts to bring rational scrutiny to theological inquiry "tend to resist logical examination and therefore are threatened with a verdict of theoretical annihilation."[49] Yet the mind continues to wonder about that which escapes its understanding, and although we know that we do not know God, we still think about what we once were taught to believe.

We are told to obey God out of fear and worship him out of love. Which is it? The painful spectacle of suffering in the world makes us wonder why a perfect Creator would create imperfect creatures. Niebuhr's contemporary, the anguished Catholic Simone Weil, saw affliction as a trial or apprenticeship. An all-wise, good, and powerful God required human beings to suffer for their moral nature. Was God a blunderer? Did the advent of Jesus as redeemer mean the Supreme Being had made such a mess of things in his first act of creation that he gave himself and humanity a second chance? To trace man's efforts to understand God is to start with theology and end with comedy.

God is the One and only One whom finite man will never know

(Augustine). He is the Supreme Being and Creator of all things and the Prime Mover who truly knows himself—"I am who I am" (Aquinas). He is the omniscient shill who invites you to roll the dice and bet your soul (Pascal). God is an "imbecile" (Herman Melville), the "deity of the sick" (Nietzsche), the oracle of "obscurity" (Walter Lippmann), an "underachiever" (Woody Allen), the presence who fails to make an appearance (Samuel Beckett).

The genius of Reinhold Niebuhr is that we can laugh with Allen and wait with Beckett and still reflect on the theologian's teachings. Niebuhr always said the knowledge of God found its validity in human experience. For a half century he would offer us his observations on the state of society and the nature of politics, taking us into the heart of history, where the self is revealed.

2

Religion:
"A Recipe for Decadence"

In 1938 the *New Republic* reviewed the intellectual life of the 1920s in a symposium that invited writers and intellectuals to identify "books that changed our minds." The texts cited most often were written by Thorstein Veblen (*The Theory of the Leisure Class, The Theory of Business Enterprise*) and Charles Beard (*An Economic Interpretation of the Constitution*), followed by Oswald Spengler (*The Decline of the West*), Sigmund Freud (*The Interpretation of Dreams*), John Dewey (*Human Nature and Conduct*), Henry Adams (*The Education of Henry Adams*), Vernon Parrington (*Main Currents in American Thought*), the *Prefaces* of George Bernard Shaw, and Alfred North Whitehead's *Science and the Modern World*. Not one of the authors was a theologian and all were doubtful that religion could be persuasive to the modern world. For the "lost generation" of writers in the 1920s, God's presence went unremarked, serious minds looked elsewhere for terms on which to live, and even romantic love was "at times only a sort of obscene joke," as Joseph Wood Krutch put it in *The Modern Temper*.[1]

In 1927 Niebuhr published his first book, *Does Civilization Need Religion?*, which urged the Christian church to undertake the moral renewal of modern society. Thoughtful people were turning away from religion, Niebuhr argued, not so much because religion was unable to compete with science in explaining the natural order but because it was failing to make civilization ethical. Religion would have to overcome moral cynicism and deterministic naturalism, and the road to its recovery lay in teaching men "to find God by loving their brothers and to love their brothers because they have found God."[2]

At this point Niebuhr did not emphasize the paradoxes of freedom and finitude, the ethic of love, and the fact of sin that are the hallmarks of his theology. Against the mordant currents of secular skepticism, he stressed the importance of conscience, love, and forgiveness. Religion would have to find a way into modern sensibilities to combat the cynicism and disillusionment that led the young to think of little but getting high and getting laid. Niebuhr abandoned any attempt at a logical argument for religion's truth claims and instead made his case by emphasizing religion's resources for ethical action in society. According to his biographer Richard Fox, "Niebuhr was a thoroughgoing Jamesian pragmatist" who believed he could salvage religion by basing it on experience, recasting it as "a message not of propositional truths, but of poetic, dramatic, 'irrational' truths."[3]

Three books appeared soon after Niebuhr's that would undercut his entreaties and leave religion in shambles. Joseph Wood Krutch's *The Modern Temper* (1929), H. L. Mencken's *Treatise on the Gods* (1930), and Walter Lippmann's *A Preface to Morals* (1929) were emblematic of the intellectuals' disillusionment with progressive and high-minded thinking. Their withering criticisms did not spare religion.

Krutch, the drama critic for the *Nation*, argued that modern civilization had crippled the human spirit. Science undermined all beliefs in right and wrong, turned reason into rationalization, and made love a function of biology. Faith was replaced by philosophy, and "then philosophy, losing all confidence in its own conclusions, begins to babble of 'beneficent fictions' instead of talking about 'Truth." Niebuhr may have thought religion could draw support from poetry and drama, but Krutch pointed out, citing Santayana, that "poetry is religion which is no longer believed."[4]

If God exists, Krutch wondered, why does man feel so alienated from him, and why is the natural universe that he created known to science only as a mechanistic structure without spirit? Pragmatists like James overcame dualism by conceiving of man as at one with nature, with the mind a product of an environment that mind itself could transform. But how could religion establish itself on the basis of felt experience? Krutch advised that we recognize the effort for what it is—"only a faint futility."[5]

The journalist H. L. Mencken delighted readers during the twenties with his sardonic observations on the imbecility of mass democracy. While philosophers like Dewey were pleading the case for civic intelligence, Mencken was deriding the "booboisie." In 1925 he had a front row seat at "the monkey trial" of "the infidel Scopes" in Dayton, Tennessee. His *Treatise on the Gods*, an exploration of the nature and evolution of religion, appeared just after the stock market crash, as Americans were starting to worry more about material deprivation than theological speculation. While Niebuhr wrestled with the problem of faith and the knowledge of God, Mencken saw the fun of it: "It is Tertullian who is credited with the motto, *Credo, quia absurdum est*. I believe because it is incredible. Needless to say, he began life as a lawyer."[6]

Niebuhr explored the paradox of "the self-imposed weakness of God," the crucified Christ who demonstrates his power through a sacrificial love that redeems mankind. But Mencken hooted that the Gospels were "the sempiternal Cinderella story, lifted to cosmic dimensions." The doctrines of the Church seemed to him voodoo and buncombe. While Jesus preached love and humility, his followers were a calculating bunch more interested in survival and success:

> The Disciples, it is apparent, harbored certain doubts to the very end; perhaps, indeed, those doubts tended to increase in the last days, after it began to be evident that Jesus could not save Himself.

One of the Twelve denied Him, another betrayed Him, and the rest
seem to have cleared out.[7]

If Mencken killed religion with laughter, Walter Lippmann
buried it with sorrow. Lippmann's *A Preface to Morals* was the lost
generation's treatise for its times, reflecting the experience of intellectuals who had liberated themselves from the authority of government, society, history, religion, and family only to be disillusioned
by their own successful rebellion. Lippmann wrote that "the acids
of modernity" had created such a strong "passion to disbelieve" that
efforts to reconstruct religion through logical inference or to derive
meaning by conceiving religion as myth and symbol were doomed
to failure. These intellectual constructions could hardly convince
those who sought a foundation for faith. "When creeds have to be
proved to the doubting they are already blighted."[8]

Lippmann presaged the poststructuralists of our time in recog-
nizing that religion has no moral authority if it is merely an argument filling a social or psychological need. "If it is true that man
creates God in his own image, it is no less true that for religious
devotion he must be unconscious of the fact. Once he knows he has
created the image of God, the reality of it vanishes like last night's
dream." Lippmann recalled Santayana's advice that "matters of religion should never be matters of controversy" because "we neither
argue with a lover about his taste, nor condemn him, if we are just,
for knowing so human a passion." But Lippmann concluded that in
the modern world the beliefs of the believer are insubstantial compared to the loves of the lover. "For what would be the plight of a
lover, if we told him that his passion was charming?—though, of
course, there might be no such lady as the one he loved."[9]

Krutch, Mencken, and Lippmann were by no means the most
daunting critics of religion. Karl Marx famously dismissed religion
as "the sigh of the oppressed creature . . . the opium of the people,"
giving false consolation to the masses for life's miseries. Max Weber argued that while productive labor gave Calvinists the worldly
evidence of their salvation, the progress of science had undermined
charismatic authority such as Jesus enjoyed, and belief in miracles

had yielded to the "disenchantment of the world." Sigmund Freud told the generation of the 1920s that human life is shaped by unconscious instinctual drives, that religious conceptions are illusions expressing secret wishes, and that belief in God is the longing for a father. And when Friedrich Nietzsche declared that "God is dead," he became a hero to writers from Mencken to Eugene O'Neill, who were drawn to his attacks on a Christian smugness that stifled sensual joys and intellectual doubts. Nietzsche's famous declaration was a battle cry in the American war on Puritanism, famously defined by the sardonic Mencken as the "haunting fear that someone, somewhere, may be happy."

Reinhold Niebuhr was entirely aware of the modern criticisms of Christianity. He understood that the acids of doubt begin with reason, and that reason can destroy faith even when used in religion's defense. Niebuhr was close to Nietzsche in regarding the arguments of liberal Christianity as so soothing and comforting that they left believers without a trouble in the world—"sinners purged of conscience and made happy in their sinning," as Mencken put it in his introduction to Nietzsche's *The Anti-Christ*. Niebuhr had no great quarrel with Nietzsche's exposure of religion as "a recipe for decadence," a disguised will to power without passion or conviction. But Nietzsche's celebration of instincts and drives—"sex, the lust to rule, selfishness"—could only unsettle the theologian. For Nietzsche the "ban of morality" would have to be lifted "if one is to liberate life."[10]

Herewith an interesting juxtaposition. The German Friedrich Nietzsche decreed that all human impulses condemned as immoral should be free from prohibition. The American Reinhold Niebuhr held that evil must be faced rather than denied, and while he viewed sex as a normal physical impulse, he discerned in politics a lust to rule and, especially in democratic politics, a selfishness disguised as disinterested public service. Nietzsche wrote that philosophy has been corrupted by "theological blood," that Christianity's moral ban on man's strongest and most basic instincts amounted to a war on nature: "The most lamentable example: the corruption of Pascal, who believed that his intellect had been destroyed by original sin whereas it was actually destroyed by Christianity!" Niebuhr, in contrast, regarded the self's assertions of ego as the very expression of pride, the conceit that engenders a lust for possession and the violence and miseries that human beings inflict upon one another. Nietzsche would release sin from social ostracism; Niebuhr saw it already released and residing in comfort in a society that accepted it with a wink and a smile. The German philosopher insisted that modern man relinquish Christianity and forswear guilt and pity in order to take the first welcome steps toward power. The American theologian insisted that modern man recover Christianity in order to accept the guilt and sorrow that accompanies the necessary use of power.

To compare Nietzsche to Niebuhr is to watch one intellect push an old world forward as the other holds a new world back from the brink. For Nietzsche the curse of Christianity was the "worm of sin" that Luther and the Reformation imposed on Europe. For Niebuhr the illusion of Christianity was liberal Protestantism's belief in humanity's goodness; its erroneous mission was to overcome ignorance, not deliver us from evil. Nietzsche thought Christianity gave civilization a bad conscience and an enfeebled will. Niebuhr thought Americans had an easy conscience and were too quick to absolve themselves of guilt. If Nietzsche's Germany was swamped by repression, Niebuhr's America skated away from responsibility.[11]

MORAL MAN AND IMMORAL SOCIETY

Reinhold Niebuhr asked more questions than he could answer. As a young pastor in Detroit, he was uncertain about his capacity to guide his congregation. His observations, jotted down and then published in 1929 as *Leaves from the Notebook of a Tamed Cynic*, were the reflections of a humble man, called to serve but hoping to lead. Niebuhr compared his state of mind on leaving the home of a dying person to that of a medical doctor. He imagined that a doctor would leave feeling satisfied that he had used all his skills and knowledge on the patient's behalf. But Niebuhr could only wonder about the solace promised by religion and its value for those thought to be most in need of it. "When called upon to bury someone whose life revealed spiritual charm and moral force I can preach the hope of immortality with conviction and power. But funerals of religious and moral nondescripts leave me enervated," he wrote in 1924. "I think I can bury a brazen sinner with more satisfaction."[12]

Niebuhr admitted that he had no easy answers to the conditions of modern life. He was stunned by what he saw of Detroit factory life, of assembly line workers numbed by mindless routine:

> We went through one of the big automobile factories today. So artificial is life that these factories are like a strange world to me though I have lived close to them for many years. The foundry interested me particularly. The heat was terrific. The men seemed weary. Here manual labor is drudgery and toil is slavery. The men cannot possibly find any satisfaction in their work. They simply work to make a living. Their sweat and dull pain are part of the price paid for the fine cars we all run. And most of us run the cars without knowing what price is being paid for them.[13]

Unlike Marx, who thought industrial capitalism would provoke alienated workers to violent revolution, or the American Thorstein Veblen, who believed the future belonged to those who understood the machinery of industrial productivity, Niebuhr reflected on the social cost of human selfishness. He knew better than to blame the workers' plight solely on Henry Ford and other titans of capitalism. A complacent middle class was also at fault; eager to acquire material goods and indifferent to the needs of the community, it withdrew into the comforts of family and counted on the church to remain silent about the worship and manipulation of wealth. To Niebuhr, American Christianity in the 1920s seemed less a theology of conviction than a cult of celebration. "A national Thanksgiving, particularly if it is meant to express gratitude for material bounty, becomes increasingly a pharisaic rite."[14]

In 1928 Niebuhr left Detroit for New York City's Union Theological Seminary, where he accepted a position teaching applied Christianity and social ethics. His reputation, based in part on his writings in the *Christian Century*, preceded him to Manhattan's

Morningside Heights, and students flocked to his lectures and chapel sermons. His provocative, brash teaching style and rumpled clothes appealed more to the students he challenged than to the faculty whose genteel proprieties he upset. Although Niebuhr attended to religion in the classroom, his deeper passions were stirred by ethical questions raised by contemporary politics and society. His students recalled sessions in their professor's office discussing Saint Augustine as his phone rang with calls from politicians and labor leaders seeking advice on current events.

A year after Niebuhr arrived at the seminary, the stock market crash shattered the Wall Street wealth machine. The Great Depression revived the American Left as the economy's collapse seemed to vindicate Marx's prediction that the bourgeoisie would produce its own "gravediggers" and that capitalism, a victim of "internal contradictions," would polarize social classes and mobilize the proletariat to seize power. Many radical writers, persuaded by Marx that class conflict would lead to violence, predicted that it was only a matter of time before revolution came to America.

As communist writers and workers were "waiting for Lefty," Niebuhr was writing a book whose implications both outraged conservatives and upset radicals. It restated an insight well understood by the framers of the Constitution but one that has eluded generations of thinkers in modern American intellectual history: Man can become moral, but society is inevitably immoral.

Niebuhr's *Moral Man and Immoral Society* appeared in 1932. In that year New York governor Franklin D. Roosevelt defeated President Herbert Hoover's bid for reelection, but for many Eastern literary intellectuals and writers it was the year they signed the manifesto "Culture and Crisis," which denounced the two major parties, condemned the weakness of the Socialist Party, and called for the election of the Communist Party ticket of William Z. Foster for president and the African American James W. Ford for vice president. Most of these writers steered clear of joining the Communist Party and refused to submit to the dictates of Moscow. What mattered to them was Marxism as a theoretical proposition. The eminent literary critic Edmund Wilson spoke for many in urging, "We must take communism away from the communists," while the philosopher Sidney Hook made a philosophical case for a uniquely American communism grounded in Marxism and pragmatism. In *Towards the Understanding of Karl Marx: A Revolutionary Interpretation* (1933), Hook presented Marxism as a philosophy of both freedom and determinism. Likening Marxism to American pragmatism, he said both subscribed to "praxis," a theory of knowledge that says the world can be understood only through taking actions that change it. At this early stage in his career, Hook actually defended the idea of proletarian dictatorship.

Niebuhr, however, showed that the case for Marxism and pragmatism was more fictional than foundational. *Moral Man and Immoral Society*, his first major book in political philosophy, discomfited Marxists and socialists during the Depression decade. While arguing for a radical engagement in politics and civic life, Niebuhr dismissed as utopian the Left's view that politics is the ultimate means for attaining social justice.

Niebuhr agreed that individuals may use their capacity for reason and their love of God to transcend their natural drives and selfish interests, but he argued that the individual conscience is lost as soon as human behavior becomes collective. Individuals can "refine and purge" their egoistic impulses, acting responsibly and benevolently toward one another, but selfishness, dishonesty, and hypocrisy invariably predominate whenever individuals organize themselves into groups, nations, classes, and races.

> In every human group there is less reason to guide and to check impulse, less capacity for self-transcendence, less ability to comprehend the needs of others and therefore more unrestrained egoism than the individuals, who compose the group, reveal in their personal relationships.[15]

Niebuhr argued that middle-class reformers, intellectuals, and liberal Protestants expected too much from reason and persuasion. They idealized the benefits of peace and assumed that humanity's cooperative social nature would emerge through moral education and civic reform. Niebuhr cited John Dewey as a prime example of someone who believed injustice could be rectified and ignorance overcome by the rational application of intelligence to "problematic situations."

No doubt reason could organize human energies, but Niebuhr warned that reason would more likely serve "the possessive instinct or the will-to-power" rather than any larger sense of social obligation. Caught up in the spirit of the 1930s, Niebuhr admitted that Marxists were justified in being cynical about the ethical pretensions of democratic reform politics. The times were ripe for worker rebellion against a privileged class unwilling to relinquish power. But he cautioned that Marxism's "deification" of social class was itself "charged with egoism and vindictiveness." Communists were "hopeless romantics" to think they could centralize power for the proletariat without creating new sources of political oppression.[16]

Marxists follow Hegel in insisting that "necessity is blind only insofar as it is not understood," and they profess to see a historical dialectic that will usher in a "realm of freedom" as the final stage of society. By contrast, Niebuhr maintained that there is an inevitable and tragic conflict between the ethical conscience of the individual and the strivings of society. He denied that humankind could transcend its sinfulness and cited Saint Augustine in asserting that what is called peace in this world must be gained by strife. "The future peace and justice of society," he noted,

> therefore depend upon, not one but many, social strategies, in all of which moral and coercive factors are compounded in varying degrees. So difficult is it to avoid the Scylla of despotism and the Charybdis of anarchy that it is safe to hazard the prophecy that the dream of perpetual peace and brotherhood for human society is one which will never be realized. It is a vision prompted by the conscience and insight of individual man, but incapable of fulfillment by collective man.[17]

A century and a half earlier the authors of the *Federalist* had taught the same lesson. The Antifederalists, those who opposed ratifying the US Constitution, had asked why a federal government should thwart the people's will by imposing on the majority an elaborate system of checks and balances. Why not rely on the people's capacity for honor, virtue, and reputation to prevent the abuse of power? The answer given by James Madison, Alexander Hamilton, and John Jay is one that Niebuhr could endorse: While the individual conscience can be made responsive to the principles of honor and the pressure for reputation, those tasked to write a constitution establishing a government must be less concerned to teach people how they ought to behave than to predict how they will behave. The *Federalist* authors recognized that "factions" indifferent to the virtues of honor and civic duty would form to realize their "interests" and that the new nation would have to take this into account if it were to govern itself wisely.

It is striking that God is mentioned four times in the Declaration of Independence but not once in the Constitution. In *Federalist* number 37, James Madison writes that pious Americans will perceive in the Constitution "a finger of that Almighty hand which has been so frequently and signally extended to our relief in the critical states of the revolution." Notice that God, who extends his hand to aid the revolutionaries, lifts only a finger to help form the new government.

The Federalists, to the chagrin of the Antifederalists, prohibited all religious tests for office and ignored a recommendation—by Benjamin Franklin—that the constitutional convention begin its sessions with a prayer. The Constitution's framers neither looked to the Almighty nor believed the virtue of the citizenry was sufficient for self-rule. Madison expected the people's representatives would naturally favor their own selfish interests and that government would have to check them. In *Federalist* number 49 he wrote:

> The *passions*, therefore, not the *reason*, of the public would sit in judgment. But it is the reason, alone, of the public, that ought to control and regulate the government. The passions ought to be controlled and regulated by the government.

How to enable reason to rule? In *Federalist* number 51 Madison stated the dilemma candidly:

> In framing a government which is to be administered by men over men, the great difficulty lies in this: you must first enable the government to control the governed, and in the next place oblige it to control itself. A dependence upon the people is, no doubt, the primary control on the government, but experience has taught mankind the necessity of auxiliary precautions.

Lacking confidence that reason and virtue could control passion and self-interest, the framers relied on the "machinery of government" rather than the morality of humanity.[18]

Niebuhr admired the *Federalist* authors for seeing the need to check power with power and for understanding that human beings are motivated mainly by self-interest—all the more so when they deny it. In *Moral Man and Immoral Society* he explored the evil in the social order and concludes that religious idealism is insufficient to overcome it or to produce a semblance of justice in society. He argued that because human collectives are "morally obtuse," the most satisfactory social arrangements will be those based on "competing assertions of interest." In place of the Christian ethic of pure love, Niebuhr proposed that "a purely prudential morality must be satisfied with something less than the best."[19]

The Founders' mistrust of religion as a guide to social conduct and political liberty has not, however, prevented Americans from looking to religion as a progressive force in politics. Martin Luther King Jr. had a realist's sense of power when he led the civil rights movement using a strategy of nonviolent demonstrations and boycotts. These were the pressure tactics of "prudential morality." "Lamentably," he wrote in his famous "Letter from a Birmingham Jail" in 1963, "it is a historical fact that privileged groups seldom give up their privileges voluntarily. Individuals may see the moral light and voluntarily give up their unjust posture; but, as Reinhold Niebuhr has reminded us, groups tend to be more immoral than individuals."[20]

3

The Closing of
the European Mind

It is through images that we seem to remember the events of World War II and the Cold War: dramatic black-and-white photos of the bloody beaches of Normandy, the ravaged streets of Stalingrad, and the joyous liberation of Paris; grainy newsreel footage of planes landing at Templehof airport to break the Berlin Blockade and of weary soldiers on the Korean peninsula. We recall aerial photos of Soviet missile sites in Cuba, color film coverage of a seemingly endless war in Vietnam, then video of the Berlin Wall being torn down in 1989 and shots of toppled statues of Lenin and Stalin symbolizing the collapse of Soviet communism.

The defeat of the Third Reich and the end of the Cold War have led many Americans to conclude that the Allied victory was due to the superiority of the "American way of life," and for that we have plenty of images in back issues of *Time* and *Life*. Henry Luce, the magazines' influential publisher, once proclaimed our era "the American century." But is it?

When we shift from histories of war to histories of ideas we lose our visual clues. The outcome of World War II was a victory for the Allies' arms, but did it mean success for their aims? And when the Berlin Wall was torn down and the Cold War ended, were Western

47

democracy and liberal capitalism vindicated? We know the end of World War I led to the collapse of liberalism and democracy on the European continent. In America it gave rise to a disenchantment with liberalism that weighed on the lost generation of the 1920s and permeated the thinking of Old Left intellectuals in the 1930s. That disenchantment has not disappeared. "The most insistent propaganda of those days," wrote the historian of ideas Isaiah Berlin, referring to the early years of World War II, "declared that humanitarianism and liberalism and democratic forces were played out, and that the choice now lay between two bleak extremes, Communism and Fascism—the red or the black."[1]

The defeat of these European ideologies, first the fall of fascism in 1945, and then the political collapse of communism after 1989, ought to have signaled the triumph of liberal democracy as the enduring political philosophy of the West. Yet doubts arose in many quarters. From the Right the classical liberal economist Friedrich Hayek warned that the bureaucratic centralization of state power that characterizes totalitarian rule would continue under conditions of democracy, and that democratic socialism was sure to undermine liberal values. Modernists who rejected any truth rooted in fixed principles found belief in liberal humanism as problematic as faith in God, and some repudiated democratic principles and adopted ideologies of the Left and Right. As for outright supporters of Nazi Germany and the Soviet Union, they remained in a state of denial. As the regimes they once backed disappeared, Marxists took refuge in the academic world while fascists retreated to Latin American hideaways. The machinery of totalitarianism was on the trash heap of history but the ideas that kept it running could still be tapped. These ideas will be exhausted only if the crimes and lies they buttress are exposed and admitted. There must be consciousness of sin before contrition, as Niebuhr well knew. But the "uneasy conscience" often allows the self to escape acknowledgment of its own motives.

How to avoid a moral and intellectual reckoning? That has been a salient characteristic of modern intellectual history, and the evidence for it is pervasive. Signs appeared soon enough, starting with the Moscow show trials of 1936–1937, where old Bolsheviks willingly confessed to subversive acts against the Soviet Union that they could not possibly have committed. By falsely admitting their guilt, dedicated Communists demonstrated their loyalty to Stalin and the party, hoping to be pardoned by history even if they first had to go before a firing squad. The Nuremberg trials of 1945–1946 offered another signal that discredited ideologies can overcome political and military disaster, as high-ranking Nazis insisted that history would redeem the Third Reich. The same belief surfaced during the trial of the Nazi Holocaust planner Adolf Eichmann in 1962–1963. The political philosopher Hannah Arendt reported Eichmann's testimony that he was simply doing his duty, following Kant's categorical imperative in authorizing the killing of millions of Jews. By carrying out his orders Eichmann believed he was fulfilling the Führer's universal command.[2]

That communists and Nazis died for their ideas, convinced they would be realized in politics and sanctioned by history, suggests there is something profoundly rotten in the German philosophy they used to justify their actions. Hegel's philosophy of history spawned opposing schools of thought. Theories of the "logic of history" entered Russia when Lenin arrived at Saint Petersburg's Finland Station in 1917, and they infected those who marched through the streets of Berlin in 1933. The German disease, so called by the political philosopher Allan Bloom in *The Closing of the American Mind* (1987), now influences postmodernism, which deconstructs and re-creates new worlds of meaning through the willful interpretation and distorting representation of texts. But in the 1940s German thought meant Kant, Hegel, Fichte, Nietzsche, Oswald Spengler, the composer Richard Wagner, and the Nazi ideologist Alfred Rosenberg. We know now that Nietzsche had little connection to Nazism, and had his sister not falsified his writings to please Hitler, the world would have learned sooner that the philosopher was a critic of anti-Semitism and scornful of German nationalism. Nietzsche would have treated the rallies of the Third Reich not as the triumph of the will but as the fear of the weak and the resentment of the inferior.

• • •

"What are the books . . . that have really impressed you and in some measure changed the direction of your thinking?" asked Malcolm Cowley in *Books That Changed Our Minds*. The liberal critic Lewis Mumford picked Oswald Spengler's *The Decline of the West*. Its sweeping judgment that Western civilization was in decay, the victim of a destructive Faustian obsession with modern technology that devitalized man and thwarted nature, has "fascinated many of our contemporaries," wrote Mumford, an "organicist" liberal opposed to bigness and bureaucracy. Spengler repudiated Hitler and anti-Semitism before his death in 1936, and, like Nietzsche, he could hardly be blamed for the rise of Nazism. But his prophecies of doom appealed to disillusioned readers, and after the dishonorable Munich conference in 1938 his words seemed to ring true, suggesting that the West had indeed entered the twilight.[3]

That perspective troubled Niebuhr, who rejected the notion that societies are organic in nature or cyclical in development. In *The Nature and Destiny of Man*, his two-volume magnum opus, Niebuhr affirmed that there is no natural necessity; societies are free to become creative or to decline, to succeed or fail to respond to new challenges, and he criticized Spengler's cycles of cultural rise and fall. His probing mind was impatient with Spengler's distinctions between vitalistic cultures (Greece and Germany) and putrefying civilizations (Rome and America).[4]

During the war years of the 1940s many Western intellectuals were as intrigued by the determinism of the German mind as Roosevelt and Churchill were preoccupied with the relentlessness of the Wehrmacht. The period saw the publication of Edmund Wilson's *To the Finland Station* (1940); Max Eastman's *Marxism: Is It Science?* (1940); Peter Viereck's *Metapolitics: From the Romantics to Hitler* (1941); Eric Fromm's *Escape from Freedom* (1941); Max Horkheimer's germinal essays published as *The End of Reason*

(1941) and his *Dialectic of Enlightenment*, coauthored with The-odor Adorno (1944); Sidney Hook's *The Hero in History* (1943); Friedrich Hayek's *The Road to Serfdom* (1944); and Karl Popper's two-volume *The Open Society and Its Enemies* (1945), whose second volume bore the subtitle *Hegel: The High Tide of Prophecy*. Each grappled with German thinking in its origins and outcomes, finding in it seeds of the authoritarian mind and the totalitarian state.

Some thinkers on the Left admired the revolutionary potential of German philosophy. Wilson's beautifully written but politically embarrassing *To the Finland Station*, subtitled *A Study in the Writing and Acting of History*, tried to demonstrate how Hegelian ideas led Marx and Lenin to change the world, while *Reason and Revolution: Hegel and the Rise of Social Theory* (1941), by the émigré scholar Herbert Marcuse, absolved Hegel of Hitler's crimes, arguing that it was a mistake to derive a psychology of reaction from a philosophy of revolution. History, as Hegel and Marx understood it, was a progressive unfolding of humanity's power and freedom. For Hegel, history was "the unfolding of Spirit in *time* as nature is the unfolding of the Idea in *space*."[5] "The Emperor—this world-soul," Hegel wrote upon watching a victorious Napoleon enter Jena in 1806. In the 1940s it seemed as if philosophy was again on the march across the battlefields of Europe, less explicated in texts than carried forward by the clash of armies.

Niebuhr was fighting his own war against Hegelian thinking. His sympathies lay with the existentialists: the subjectivist Kier-kegaard, Hegel's great nemesis; Nietzsche, who exposed the hypocrisies of liberal rationalism; and Heidegger, who, to the extent that his views were then understood, showed how existence creates anxiety as humankind is "thrown" into the world. Niebuhr rejected any determinist theory of history; his goal was to save history from Hegel—and steep it in sin. Because most of the momentous events of history, the wars fought and empires won, were built on a desire for power and a pride in possession, the deceits and self-deceits of humanity had to be exposed. How, he wondered, could religion appeal to the conscience if the claims of history continually excused terror and violence as mere side-effects of an inevitable destiny propelled by reason or the proletariat or the master race?

The absorption of religion, philosophy, literature, and science into the study of history has come to be known as "historicism." The historicist believes all moral and political standards are relative and must be understood in the context of their time, which can give rise to a radical relativism about morality and political values, an attitude that prevails today among many postmodernists. However, some versions of historicism move beyond relativism, arguing that an intellectual vanguard can become so aware of the context affecting its values that it can transcend its own limiting conditions, take charge of its place in history, and shape its future. At the "end of history" the realized self, embodied in a "world-historical individual" (Hegel's Napoleon), a race, or a social class, will achieve its destiny by becoming the object of its own awareness.

Karl Popper, who would explore the power of this vision in his book *The Poverty of Historicism*, recalled the hold it had on his generation:

> During my studies in Vienna, the climate in right-wing and left-wing circles was strongly historicistic. "History is with us" was a cry you could hear from National Socialists and the many closely related groups, as well as from Social Democrats to whom I and my friends belonged. "Scientific socialism" was the scientific proof that socialism was bound to come, whatever may happen. But the opponents on the right had similar ideas about history. The various nationalist and fascist parties took over much of the Marxist (especially of the Communist) ideology and turned it, dialectically, into a strikingly similar mirror image.[6]

Most political observers during the war years missed the meaning of this development. They interpreted the rise of totalitarianism in Europe as a political event, the product of actions taken by demagogues possessed by a terrifying lust for power. Some American conservatives even convinced themselves that the New Deal was as great a menace as communism and fascism. But critics of "scientific socialism" like Popper, his friend the Austrian economist Friedrich Hayek, and the ex-Marxist Sidney Hook rejected the historicism of the Left and the Right and grounded their objections in the logic of scientific inquiry. They would reach distinctly different conclusions: Hayek's thesis that central government planning was the first step on the road to collectivism appealed to conservatives; Popper argued that incremental, "piecemeal" social engineering could protect democratic government through empirical trial-and-error reforms; and Hook abandoned his earlier support for radicalism and revolution to champion pragmatism and democracy. Each appealed to science and logic to dismantle the myth of historical destiny and the Hegelian state.

In contrast, Niebuhr brought his understanding of religion to bear on the struggle against totalitarianism. He insisted that what stood in the way of democracy was pride, righteousness, and self deception. Philosophers and economists might dismiss religion as prescientific, and Marxists would explain that religion loses its mystery once it is understood as a natural outcome of the conditions producing it, but to Niebuhr religion was a powerful antidote to the poison of self-regard. As a body of wisdom, Christianity could illuminate how and why men and nations inflict violence upon each other. Religion could teach humankind to remember what it struggles to forget: the indelible stain of sin that imprisons the self in its own finitude.

THREE WORLD OUTLOOKS: CLASSICAL, MODERN, ROMANTIC

Niebuhr's two-volume Gifford lectures dealt with nothing less than "the nature and destiny of man," contrasting a "Christian interpretation" to three rival visions: the classic outlook of ancient Greece and Rome; modern views, extending from the fourteenth to the eighteenth centuries; and nineteenth-century Romanticism. Each epoch, wrote Niebuhr, suffered from an epistemological fallacy, the illusion that the human capacity for knowledge is self-sufficient. This illusion, the most fundamental and most constant in history, found expression in both Nazism's cult of the irrational and communism's myth of scientific materialism.

Niebuhr explained that in the classical view of Plato, Aristotle, and the Stoics, reason comprehends the natural order of things and brings the mind into harmony with the soul and close to God. The passions, when not restrained and disciplined by the teachings of the ancient philosopher, are subjects for the dramatist, who enacts their tragic consequences. However, history has no meaning because it consists of nothing but contingent events that come to be and pass away, defying the eternal truths. Christianity, by contrast, unifies body and soul under the sovereignty of God and history acquires meaning. It conceives of history as both universal—a destiny beyond time and nature made possible by the revelation of Christ—and temporal—the actions of finite creatures of God ensnared in the inherited burden of sin.

If the ancients were "tempted to melancholy" while contemplating life's brevity, the moderns were optimists about man's capacity for reason and virtue. Niebuhr identified belief in progress, trust in reason and science, and the worship of genius and originality as constants in the intellectual history of Europe from the Renaissance to the Enlightenment. He praised the humanists and scientists for their discoveries but warned that it was a mistake for the Renaissance to free the human spirit from the need for grace and for the Enlightenment to expect human reason to be a sufficient guarantee of virtue. By conceiving of man as a dualism of mind and body, Descartes, "the fountain source of modern culture," had focused the mind on the mastery of nature and the scrutiny of its own reasoning powers. Human invention and industrial productivity flourished, but the quest to know God languished. Capitalism and Marxism, rival ideologies of progress and power, pushed aside the awareness of life's transience and the striving for its transcendence that were the hallmarks of Christian endeavor.[7]

Romanticism, the third major perspective, posited the creative power of emotion and the imagination against reason's emphasis on logic and universality. Niebuhr found vital Romantic qualities in Nietzsche's "form-defying ambitions and lusts of the spirit," but he warned that Nietzsche allowed nothing to stand in the way of the will to power and that his delight in exposing hypocrisy had unfortunate political implications:

> Nietzsche's understanding of the hidden lie, of man's capacity for self-deception, relates him not only to Marx and Freud but to the Christian conception of original sin. But a tentative affinity of thought at this point is quickly transmuted into conflict when Nietzsche seeks to overcome the hidden lie by the robust and "honest" lie. This element in Nietzsche's thought is partly responsible for the brazen dishonesty of contemporary fascist politics. It is needless to point out that the "honest" lie represents no real gain. The dishonest pretensions of human nature are not cured by disavowing the value of truth. We solve no problems by disavowing values to which we are only partially loyal and for which we must pretend a greater loyalty than we can actually give.[8]

Nietzsche was a savant without a solution. While the search for truth may yield illusions, the philosopher who disavows the search will create his own illusions.

During the early 1940s it was common among political philosophers and intellectual historians to argue that fascism was a product of German Romanticism but that Marxism was rooted in the Enlightenment's belief in science and reason. Niebuhr rejected this opinion. He understood that Marxism had appropriated Hegelian "reason," turning the chaos of history into destiny through class struggle. However, Niebuhr's immediate concern was Nazism, and so he focused his criticisms on the German Romantics and Idealists who rejected the Christian concept of the inherited "fall" and sought to submerge the self in the universality of history. The Romantic sources for the loss of the self were many, including Nietzsche, who replaced the primacy of the mind with the will to power; Schopenhauer, who substituted an undifferentiated and unified will for the will of many; Schiller, who invoked aesthetics as a weapon of political emancipation; and Schleiermacher, who submerged the individuality of the person into the individuality of the nation. Hitler had almost endowed Nazism with intellectual foundations when he appealed to such notions in *Mein Kampf*, where he announced that the "patriot" leaves philosophy behind "to seek the 'life forces,' the irrational impulses which seem to him more characteristic of the German mind."[9]

Niebuhr's view seemed to find support in the work of the young American poet-historian Peter Viereck, who explored the origin of these "life forces" in *Metapolitics: From the Romantics to Hitler* (1941). Viereck's argument that Nazism could claim roots in nineteenth-century Romanticism provoked a sharp dissent from the historian Jacques Barzun, whose book *Darwin, Marx, Wagner: Critique of a Heritage* appeared the same year. Barzun insisted that fascism was a revolt against the Western heritage, but Viereck had a supporter in the novelist Thomas Mann. Rejecting Barzun's argument that politics seldom embodies the course of ideas, the author of *The Magic Mountain* commended Viereck and acknowledged the links between the Germany of Wagner and the Germany of Hitler as "intricate and painful interrelationships which undeniably exist."[10]

Niebuhr agreed that fascism concerned ideas far more than the politics of the Versailles treaty or the economics of the Depression. He had no doubt that Nazism had its origins in Romanticism, which he defined as the view that biological and subrational forces shape human thought and action to determine the course of history. Romanticism was as misconceived as rationalism:

> If rationalism tends to depreciate the significance, power, inherent order and unity of biological impulses, romanticism tends to appreciate these without recognizing that human nature knows no animal impulse in its pure form.[11]

What Romanticism missed was a recognition that the self contains a sense of finitude as well as the capacity for freedom. The self, noted Niebuhr, mediates between mind and body, spirit and nature, embodying its sins and temptations but also its virtues and freedom. Niebuhr cited the sexual drive as an example of an impulse in the self that is more than nature and less than spirit, a pure need hedged with temptations and prohibitions. "The difficulty which man experiences in bringing his various impulses into some kind of harmony is therefore not caused by the recalcitrance of nature but occasioned by the freedom of spirit." Romanticism made the mistake of seeking a total unity of experience and nature, which at worst "anticipates the anti-semitism of modern German fascism."[12]

KNOWLEDGE AND THE PROBLEM OF POWER

Intellectual historians often mark World War II as a crossroads for modernity. Some, like Viereck, portray fascism as a tidal wave of irrational Romanticism that crashed against Western liberalism, the great bulwark against tyranny. Others, however, have noted that even as the wave of Romanticism crested, support for liberalism was already weakening. While liberalism was still applauded as a way of governing, more and more thinkers considered it defective as a way of thinking. The many strands of modern scientific thought—naturalism, pragmatism, historicism, Darwinism, Marxism—devised methods for reason to obtain knowledge, but all denied that what resulted was synonymous with truth, or that truth could withstand the transformations of history. Modern thinkers were doubters. They did not think it was possible to establish a universal criterion for truth in morals, politics, and science.

During the years before the United States entered World War II Niebuhr was deeply engaged in the struggle against political tyranny. Dismayed by the pacifism of the Socialist Party, outraged by the cynical 1939 Nazi-Soviet nonaggression pact, and grateful for President Roosevelt's support for Great Britain in the war on Nazism, Niebuhr was disinclined to evaluate American politics in the harsh terms he presented in *Moral Man and Immoral Society* in 1932. The major political debate in the early 1940s was where America stood on the war against fascism. Niebuhr's most pressing concern was to establish a firm intellectual foundation in support of the advocates for intervention.

A great debate between the isolationists and the interventionists erupted, and grew in intensity as each side attacked the other's response to the world crisis. Some interventionists eagerly blamed relativism in modern thought for failing to prepare Americans to face Hitler. Niebuhr's friends, the writers Lewis Mumford and Waldo Frank, sounded the alarm against what they considered the expediency of pragmatism. With John Dewey's 1939 antiwar article "No Matter What Happens—Stay Out" clearly in mind, Mumford responded in 1940 with an essay, "The Corruption of Liberalism," in the *New Republic*. Mumford argued that pragmatism had sullied an "ideal liberalism" that drew its strength from classical human-ism and universal moral values. Pragmatism's rational problem-solving way of looking at the world gingerly sidestepped the need to condemn the immorality of Nazism and to issue a call to arms against it. In "Our Guilt in Fascism," Waldo Frank added that "em-pirical rationalism," a belief in science and calculating reason, led to a "modernist solipsist religion of things and words." The University of Chicago scholastic Mortimer Adler similarly attacked positivism and naturalism for separating facts from values, and scientific rea-soning from ultimate ends. He urged Americans to seek out an edu-cation in the "Great Books" of Western civilization, especially Aris-totle and Aquinas, whose metaphysical account of first principles and final causes would protect democracy from godless fascism. All this was too much for Dewey's defender Sidney Hook, who orga-nized a 1943 symposium in the *Partisan Review* titled "The New Failure of Nerve." Its participants argued that in a time of crisis what American democracy needed was empirical knowledge, not antiquated philosophical presuppositions.[13]

Niebuhr understood that this debate was not merely about liber-alism's capacity to instill values or pragmatism's ability to prepare Americans to deal with totalitarianism. What had to be faced was what he considered the inadequacy of liberal ideas about man and society to answer this question: How can one know what is morally wrong without knowing what is objectively right?

In Western history the answers to this question had often come from authorities—the authority of religion, demanding submis-sion to the creeds of the church, and the authority of rulers, urg-ing obedience to the laws of the state. Voices of authority promised to still the anxieties that attend the human condition and answer questions of right and wrong by offering the Christian hope of redemption or the glory of participating in a nation's historic destiny.

Then, little more than a century and a half ago, Marxism opened Western eyes to a different conception of the human condition, one that focused on the nature of ownership and possession. Seventeenth-century liberals like John Locke had explained how the impulse to acquire and hold property eases the burdens of life, but Karl Marx argued that private property made life harder to bear, and that the burden was worse for some than for others. There had always been inequalities in possession and conflicts between classes of possessors, but before Marx and the industrial revolution those who wrote about these things concentrated on rivalries between and within groups, how decisions were made, and what happened when leaders were replaced. From Homer to Shakespeare and Hume the job of history was to describe plots, rebellions, and the death of kings, oracles consulted, women abducted, and the ignominy of surrender. But Marx made history itself the vehicle for transforming society. Communism would emerge, explained the ex-Marxist Max Eastman, as workers and revolutionaries traveled "toward that society in a world which is like a moving stairway taking them the way they walk."[14]

In *The Nature and Destiny of Man* Niebuhr gave himself over to the fullness of intellectual history, to fundamental ideas, their nature and history. He was critical of the sufficiency of ancient philosophy, skeptical of the optimism of modern rationalism, and troubled by the cult of the natural in Romantic thought, especially in its relation to fascism and the course of World War II. However, only toward the very end of his study did Niebuhr mention property, an issue that had earlier preoccupied him in *Moral Man and Immoral Society*.

Western liberalism remained on trial. As World War II gave way to the Cold War it became apparent there would be no lasting peace. With the Wehrmacht in retreat and the Red Army on the offensive, Niebuhr had to redirect his attention back to the question of property and power.

. . .

Late in 1944 Niebuhr published *The Children of Light and the Children of Darkness*, a penetrating analysis of the errors of Western political and social theory. In it, he concentrated his criticism on the main currents of Western intellectual history. His analysis mostly ignored the "children of darkness," shrewd but evil moral cynics like Hitler and Stalin who "know no law beyond their will and interest." What most interested Niebuhr were the "children of light," those "who seek to bring self-interest under the discipline of a more universal law and in harmony with a more universal good." These were the great moral and social thinkers of the West who attempted to define the conditions for establishing peace and justice among nations.[15]

Instead of extolling their idealism, however, Niebuhr surprised his readers by observing that the most notable attribute of these thinkers was their "stupidity." By this he meant the pride of secular liberal idealists who were "foolish" enough to believe they knew how to overcome the tensions between the individual and the community and realize the dream of a world without conflict. Counted among the children of light were John Locke and Adam Smith, Thomas Jefferson and Tom Paine, who conceived the social contract as an effort to institutionalize the conditions for sustaining a natural harmony between the individual's self-interest and the general welfare. Niebuhr argued that a liberalism so conceived was blind to the forces of darkness. Demonic fascism refuted the innocent belief that an "invisible hand" offered an "easy resolution" to conflicts over material interests. While he admitted that liberal social theory and market economics freed humankind from feudal restrictions and remained a useful barrier to government excess, Niebuhr dismissed talk of a "free market" as the ideology of corporate interests promoting "the false individualism of middle class life."

Niebuhr was just as caustic about Marxist theorists who predicted the end of inequality and class division once property ownership was socialized and power exercised through the collective will of the people. Lenin's seizure of power in Russia might be considered a "provisionally cynical" act, but Niebuhr counted the Russian revolutionary among the children of light because he imagined that the need for force would vanish after an anarchistic Marxist millennium took shape.

Both liberals and Marxists were "children of light" because they proposed theories of rights and property to protect the individual from the unjust exercise of power. But, Niebuhr complained, both failed to understand the principal source of unjustly exercised power. Returning to his fundamental premise, he identified individual and collective self-interest and the power of self-will as the root of all evil, the original sin.

These illusions are the perfect fruits of the stupidity of the children of light and reveal the affinities, under the differences, between Marxist and bourgeois universalism. Bourgeois property theory has no safeguard against the power of individual property; and Marxist theory has no protection against the excessive power of those who manipulate a socialized economic process or who combine control of both the economic and the political process.[16]

The subtitle of *The Children of Light and the Children of Darkness* is *A Vindication of Democracy and a Critique of Its Traditional Defense*. For Niebuhr, the problem with the "traditional defense" of democracy was the theoretical treatment of what he called "the property issue" and "the questions of possessions"—economic markets, legal rights, and the role of the state. Both liberals and Marxists proposed flawed theories of how to secure social justice for the individual in relation to the community. Whatever the merits or mistakes of Locke's theory of natural rights or Marx's theory of social class, Niebuhr believed the modern intellectual history of the West had misdiagnosed the problem of power. There was no way to disentangle power and freedom from one another. What really mattered was the need to locate "the ultimate sources of the moral standards from which political principles are derived." Those sources were in religion.[17]

The onset of the Cold War was marked by a worldwide struggle for power, with the potential use of nuclear weapons at risk in every action and reaction. Niebuhr believed that while America was struggling to defend democracy against totalitarianism, it also faced a challenge to its understanding of the meaning of democracy, one that he proposed to fight in the realm of ideas. His thesis was stated most succinctly in the foreword to *Children of Light*: "Man's capacity for justice makes democracy possible, but man's inclination to injustice makes democracy necessary."[18]

As much as he believed religion was the source of morality, Niebuhr did not give up on reason. He was convinced that the mind was needed to tame power and to confront the pretensions to virtue that always promise but fail to overcome power. In an age of conflict there would be a place for both reason and religion.

THE INTELLECTUAL DIMENSIONS OF THE COLD WAR

The American people danced in the streets in May and August 1945, celebrating first the collapse of the Third Reich and then the unconditional surrender of Japan. But the end of World War II did not usher in an era of peace. Conflicts quickly surfaced to shape a new political reality. American intellectuals on the noncommunist Left were hardly surprised by the outbreak of what was soon termed the Cold War. Many, including Niebuhr, had fought the Stalinists for years and knew that a revival of democratic politics was the last thing the Kremlin wanted, but most Americans were shocked by the sudden descent, in 1946, of what Winston Churchill called an "Iron Curtain" across Europe. There followed an unprecedented series of events that thrust America into a position of world leadership: President Truman declared that the United States would aid Greece and Turkey to "contain" communism (1947); the Marshall Plan promised billions of dollars in American aid for the economic recovery of western Europe (1948); the NATO military alliance was formed to counter America's former ally, the Soviet Union (1949);

the Soviets detonated their own atomic bomb (1949); and Nationalist China fell to the Red Army of Mao Tse-Tung (1950).

If Americans were alarmed by the turn of events and anxious about the scope of their country's increased commitments, many Europeans were likewise uncertain about America's willingness to carry them out. NATO's creation disturbed those who remembered that an isolationist America, reluctant to be drawn into global crises, had failed to intervene when Nazi Germany invaded their countries. Now they wondered how the United States would respond if Soviet ground forces moved westward. If America were to rely on air power and the threat of the atomic bomb, the ensuing war could devastate Europe. Nonetheless, for protection noncommunist Europe and much of Asia looked to the United States, a country that seemed to have escaped the ongoing tragedies of world history.

Niebuhr could only wonder how America would respond to this unprecedented burden of history. Having lived through both world wars, he knew that his country was not inclined to go to war for high principles and moral purposes, but that once it was at war, moral reasons—or, more accurately, rationalizations—were the only motives it would admit. To fight is to be right, and it was disloyal to be a conscientious objector to one's country's wars. Aware of finite man's infinite capacity for self-deceit, Niebuhr explained how the power unleashed by patriotism can destroy the selflessness that is prompted by religion and that finds genuine expression in patriotism:

There is an ethical paradox in patriotism which defies every but the most astute and sophisticated analysis. The paradox is that patriotism transmutes individual unselfishness into national egoism. Loyalty to the nation is a high form of altruism when compared with lesser loyalties and more parochial interests. It therefore becomes the vehicle of all altruistic impulses and expresses itself, on occasion, with such fervor that the critical attitude of the individual toward the nation and its enterprises is almost completely destroyed. The unqualified character of this devotion is the very basis of the nation's power and of the freedom to use power without moral restraint. Thus the unselfishness of individuals makes for the selfishness of nations.[19]

Niebuhr publicly denounced the atomic bombings of Hiroshima and Nagasaki in August 1945 as a sin against the law of God and the people of Japan. But he soon qualified his protest, acknowledging that the bombings saved lives that would have been lost in a land invasion, and he noted that the United States had developed the atomic bomb out of fear that Hitler's Germany would perfect it first and use it against the Allies. Niebuhr did not endorse the "Ban the Bomb" movement—he believed atomic weapons showed only how the forces of evil could make use of technology—but he endorsed a proposal that the United States make a "solemn covenant" never to use the hydrogen bomb first.[20] Anticipating initiatives that President Ronald Reagan would implement more than three decades later, Niebuhr urged the United States to engage in personal diplomacy to negotiate nuclear disarmament with the Soviet Union. Would Niebuhr have approved of Reagan's speech calling the Soviet Union "the focus of evil in the modern world"? Moralistic Americans typically say they prepare for war for the sake of peace, but Niebuhr, imbued with the idea of original sin, worried that his country's motives were neither so pure nor so simple.

We know that the more than four-decade-long Cold War between the Soviet Union and the United States was a product of suspicion, fear, and ideology. Neither wanted what occurred, but both mistakenly feared that the other's rapid military buildup signaled a strategy of conquest, especially after Russia detonated an atomic bomb in 1949.[21] The Truman administration convinced itself that the Soviet occupation of eastern Europe was the first step toward communist expansion into western Europe. And when the communist movements that spearheaded the wartime antifascist resistance grew in political strength and popular support at the end of the war, even in Catholic countries like France and Italy, America grew alarmed at the specter of worldwide communism. With eastern Europe behind the Iron Curtain and the land mass of Asia under the Red

Star of Chinese communism, the United States felt itself gravely threatened, especially after a rapid demobilization left US ground forces no match for their rivals. Advised by Secretary of State Dean Acheson and Paul Nitze of the National Security Council, President Harry Truman intentionally exaggerated Soviet nuclear capacities and discounted those of the United States in order to "bludgeon" the government "and scare the hell" out of Congress.

Niebuhr closely followed these political developments and made his views known in a torrent of speeches and articles during the early years of the Cold War. Colleagues found it hard to keep up with his activities. He joined a State Department tour to Germany concerned with the reform of its university system, gave testimony urging the British Labour government to open Palestine to Jewish refugees, traveled throughout western Europe giving lectures on political and social reconstruction, advised the newly formed World Council of Churches on Christianity's responsibilities to the world, and participated in the formation of a new liberal anticommunist organization, Americans for Democratic Action (ADA), to ward off resurgent Republicans and reclaim the banner of liberalism from progressives sympathetic to the Soviet Union.

The ADA was established in January 1947 after the Republicans took control of Congress for the first time since 1930. In large measure, however, the group was a response to a greater challenge from the left. Former vice president Henry Wallace (who missed becoming president when Roosevelt replaced him with Missouri senator Harry Truman as the Democrats' 1944 vice-presidential nominee) had grown increasingly critical of President Truman's policies; he was convinced that the administration's truculence would only harden Stalin's rule and sow deeper suspicions that would prevent any settlement of postwar differences. Wallace spoke out against Truman's "get tough" policy toward the Soviet Union and quickly built a popular following, including support from the American Communist Party and its "fellow travelers," that led to his selection as the presidential candidate of the newly formed Progressive Party in the 1948 elections.

Niebuhr rejected the Progressives' assertions that the Soviet

Union had occupied eastern Europe only to protect its own national security. He argued instead that Marxist dogmatism had created paranoia in communist regimes against any opposition, a mentality that had led a monomaniacal Stalin to purge and execute any perceived enemy, from old Bolshevik comrades to the scientists and generals vital to Russia's future. As a member of the ADA national board, Niebuhr approved Truman's initial policy of "patience and firmness" toward the Soviets.

The ADA resolved to exclude American communists and communist sympathizers from its ranks. However, in trying to maintain a delicate balance between its commitments to civil liberties and to anticommunism, ADA members faced difficult questions. Should the American Communist Party be treated as a legitimate political party or as the covert agent of a foreign power? Such quandaries seemed to play into the hands of the supporters of Wisconsin Republican senator Joseph McCarthy, who in the early 1950s launched a red scare. With Americans subpoenaed to testify before congressional committees about "un-American" remarks and activities, a great fear gripped America, security took precedence over liberty, and the right to express one's own opinions became a cultural casualty of the Cold War.

Niebuhr disdained "McCarthyism," which saw communism as a subversive internal conspiracy rather than an overseas political threat. He doubted that Stalin intended to order the Red Army to invade western Europe, and, in contrast to conservative thinkers such as James Burnham, author of *Containment or Liberation?* (1952), he believed that there was nothing the United States could do to "roll back" the Soviet empire. Much like Winston Churchill, Niebuhr accepted the postwar division of Europe into "spheres of influence," but he was adamant in seeking to halt further Soviet expansion. The West's greatest danger was the growing popularity of communism in France, Italy, and western Germany, as well as among American liberals.

Niebuhr displayed a cool prudence about the dangers of communism, but the American media seized upon his speeches and writings to dramatize his antagonism toward the rising superpower in the East. Publisher Henry Luce was delighted to feature Niebuhr's bald pate and penetrating eyes against a background of dark clouds on the cover of *Time*'s March 8, 1948, issue, the twenty-fifth anniversary of the magazine's founding. The accompanying story observed that "Reinhold Niebuhr's new orthodoxy is the oldtime religion put through the intellectual wringer." Written by senior editor Whittaker Chambers (who would rivet the nation later in the year by accusing former New Deal official Alger Hiss of communism and espionage), the article described Niebuhr's appearance ("hawk-nosed and saturnine"), summarized his theological ideas and foreign policy views, and hailed him as the voice of "faith for a Lenten age." The Luce publications *Time* and *Life* and other popular magazines would prominently feature Niebuhr, typically depicting him as a firm Christian and defender of Western freedoms. The late 1940s and early 1950s were a tense period in history when intellectuals in many countries faced off against one another in debating democracy, communism, and the bomb. The time was ripe for Niebuhr. As his biographer Richard Fox has observed, "The culture created a spokesman for the tragic sense of life; Niebuhr had the intellectual skill, religious credentials, and personal charisma to step forward and seize the day."[22]

That description accurately captures Niebuhr's image as a cold warrior, which was invoked decades later, first by opponents of the Vietnam War and then by supporters of the Iraq War. Niebuhr was understood to be, for better or worse, a hardheaded realist who rallied support for Truman's militant foreign policies. But Fox's critical description deserves scrutiny. In his biography, Fox reprimanded Niebuhr for describing Karl Barth's neutralism on Cold War politics as "obliquely pro-Communist," and he impatiently chided Niebuhr for being more anxious about Republicans and communists than about the emerging issues of technology and mass society:

> Niebuhr was on the verge of arguing that the real danger in America was not a backward-looking libertarianism, but a new social order based on intricate systems of political and technological control. . . . But he was so wrapped up in the rearguard defense

of New Deal pragmatism against right-wing Republican dreams
of free enterprise that he did not dwell on the threat posed by the
centralizing forces in modern life."[23]

Niebuhr had no need to be reminded of the perils of modern politics and technology, and Fox is mistaken to think he "did not dwell"
on them, as if he were so intent upon boosting the Democratic Party
and the ADA that he forgot about the will to power. Niebuhr knew
that capitalism thrives on power and possession, which is why he
supported the New Deal's economic interventions and liberal welfare programs. However, he could no more deny the modern state's
threat to centralize power than he could the omnipresence of sin.

The notion that humankind is threatened by "the centralizing
forces of modern life" has been a preoccupation of both the Left and
the Right. The Left is alarmed that globalism and consumer capitalism are absorbing civil society, while conservatives worry over
"big government" takeovers. In the eighteenth century, the framers
of the Constitution thought the best way to preserve freedom was
to create political structures that oppose interest to interest. Social
and economic competition and government "checks and balances"
would prevent a concentration of power. But for modern thinkers
of all political stripes the progress of society and the direction of
history move inexorably toward the rational integration of power.
In communist societies the party dominates; in capitalist societies
the market concentrates. Niebuhr had no need to be reminded of
these "centralizing forces of modern life." He well understood that
contending political and ideological groups were bent on taking
possession of them.

While he was a biting critic of "the children of light," Niebuhr
was never guilty of what has come to be called the fallacy of "moral
equivalence," the claim that America and the Soviet Union were
so alike in their love of power and centralization that they must
be equally condemned by the same moral yardstick. Sidney Hook
rejected moral equivalency but couldn't help taking a swipe at
Niebuhr:

That simple equation between the regime of total cultural and political terror in the Soviet Union and the imperfect democracies in the West was so preposterous that even those under the sway of Niebuhrian theology—according to which all of us are infected with imperialist pride and sinful absolutism—could not swallow it.[24]

Hook was off the mark; the proper object of his scorn was the Swiss theologian Karl Barth, for whom God was so transcendent that he took no notice of worldly injustices. Still, Hook had a point: "Even if no one is completely free of guilt or sin, it does not follow that all are equally guilty or sinful. Because no one is omniscient, it does not follow that there is no difference between the informed and the ignorant."[25]

In truth, both Left and Right are too fond of claiming that freedom succumbs to centralizing forces of power and domination. It is not only right-wing Republicans but left-wing radicals, not only the Austrian school of economics but the Frankfurt school of poststructuralism, that regards totalitarianism as the inevitable outgrowth of a centralized bureaucratic state. Is their pessimism justified by history? Fox's valuable biography of Niebuhr appeared in 1985, several years before the fall of the Berlin Wall and the collapse of communism. Ironically, what made the fall of communism possible was precisely an authoritarian state's centralization of power. It is only because a few leaders in the Soviet system, especially Mikhail Gorbachev and Eduard Shevardnadze, made key decisions that communism in eastern Europe and the Soviet Union lost control of its fate and exited history with neither a war nor a revolution. Rather than render communism irreversible, bureaucratic centralization helped it collapse.

Alexis de Tocqueville predicted such a development. In *L'Ancien Regime et la Revolution*, the French thinker described how the centralization of power can lead to either revolution or counterrevolution. The French Revolution, he noted, occurred only after the *ancien regime* centralized power in the seventeenth and eighteenth centuries, depriving the provinces of their feudal rights and opening the way to a further consolidation of power when the Estates General was reconstituted as a National Assembly. With power concentrated in the court and capital, the Revolution needed only to control Paris to succeed.

In *L'Ancien Regime* Tocqueville explained how the state can either liberate or oppress society; in *Democracy in America* he explained how society can both liberate and frustrate the self. Even when the machinery of government divides and balances power, checking interest against interest as the Constitution's framers intended, society can still impose a tyranny of the majority and stifle the urge to speak truth to power.

German philosophy sustained both communism and fascism by imagining the state as the agent of history-as-reason revealing the laws immanent within itself. But Tocqueville and Niebuhr understood that the problem of history is not the "unfolding" of reason. The problem of history is society itself and the alienation of society's "democratic soul." The true drama of human history is the history of liberalism. Humanity is finite but free, corrupt but knowing, self-deceiving but determined to transcend its limitations. The fundamental problem facing the West is not the growth of the state, or the control of property, or inequality and class struggle. It is human nature itself, the presence of sin and the deceits of pride.

NIEBUHR AND THE REALIST SCHOOL OF DIPLOMACY

"War is a stern teacher," wrote Thucydides in his history of the Peloponnesian war twenty-four hundred years ago. So it was for Reinhold Niebuhr, who lived through a half dozen wars—World Wars I and II, the Spanish civil war, the wars in Korea and Vietnam, and what seemed an unending Cold War—never enjoying the prospect of a peaceful world of freedom and justice. Niebuhr's critics would say he had no one to blame but himself: he supported the interventionists before World War II and urged America to take strong stands against the Soviet Union after the war ended. Worse, he and his colleagues on the old anticommunist Left exacerbated Cold War tensions by advancing a doctrine of statecraft called "diplomatic realism."

In literature, painting, and philosophy, realism refers to a form of knowledge, to a capacity to clearly recognize what exists independent of our thoughts and wishes. In politics, realism has a similar implication: we are to see the world as it is and not as it ought to be. Against the promises of religion and philosophy, realism reminds us of the inevitability of conflict and the inefficacy of reason to restrain it. Realism may be compatible with Marx (economics as the driving force of history) and Machiavelli (politics as the expression of power), but when Marx appeals to class consciousness and Machiavelli calls for civic virtue we may question whether their appraisals of human nature are realistic. Unlike many classical and Christian thinkers, realists are reluctant to engage in ethical contemplation and moral recrimination. They are more interested in survival than salvation. The proof of realism is not love or truth but historical experience.

Niebuhr was a realist because he was religious. He accepted that humankind is selfish, willful, vindictive, and destructive, and he held that these traits were the consequence of original sin, the bitter fruit of Adam and Eve's trespass against the will of God. This was the ancient theological doctrine that Niebuhr introduced into modern political discourse, one that astounded his contemporaries, both secular and religious.[26] His meditations on international relations were shaped by the crises of World War II and the Cold War, by questions of intervention and confrontation. Critics have complained that the Cold War anticommunists could never make up their minds whether they were pragmatists or idealists. The criticism is reasonable. A pragmatist requires of politics that it answer the question: Does it work? The idealist asks: Is it right? There is a tragic dimension to realism, as Niebuhr was well aware, arising from man's compulsion to critically evaluate his own actions and to recognize his mistakes, often when it is too late to rectify them.

Niebuhr asked Americans to consider the possible necessity of war but also to challenge the conditions under which they would accept that necessity. Unlike John Foster Dulles, President Eisenhower's secretary of state, and the postwar Republican Right, Niebuhr recoiled from an American triumphalism that would brandish nuclear weaponry and threaten "massive retaliation" against Soviet aggression. Niebuhr wanted Americans to face the tragedy of inescapable conflict, not relish the pride of inevitable victory. The mission of US foreign policy was to avoid catastrophe, not claim success. Niebuhr's idea of diplomatic realism called on Americans to practice Christian charity, to seek justice and show mercy, to reject the sin of righteousness, and to regard those living under communism not as enemies but as subjects contending with a world not of their making.

Not everyone who saw himself as a "realist" in foreign affairs followed Niebuhr's counsel. Indeed, in the policy proposals of Hans Morgenthau, Walter Lippmann, and George Kennan, three of the most celebrated Cold War strategists, diplomatic realism could reach strikingly different conclusions.[27]

Niebuhr has been accused of cloaking his positions in religion. But other thinkers took positions similar to his without benefit of theological argument. In *Politics among Nations* (1947), University of Chicago professor Hans Morgenthau agreed with Niebuhr that humans are incorrigibly selfish and lust after power. But he held that their defects have less to do with evil than with the incompatibility of ethics and politics, integrity and success. Influenced by the German thinker Max Weber, Morgenthau noted that international relations is a struggle between states for dominance. America's problem was that it lost sight of power politics and forgot that nations uphold treaties only when it is in their interest to do so. Like Niebuhr, Morgenthau criticized the Truman administration's foreign policy for extending the Cold War to Asia, where the legacy of European colonialism, more than Russian imperialism or Marxist ideology, prompted revolutionary activities. Unlike Niebuhr, however, Morgenthau advocated a crash program of immediate rearmament as he watched the Soviet Union develop nuclear weapons, and he anticipated later advocates of deterrence in believing that maintaining nuclear superiority would keep Russia from attacking the West. The doctrine of deterrence and its corollary, "mutual assured destruction" (MAD), may indeed have forestalled a nuclear exchange, but it did not end the Cold War. That took President Reagan, who renounced MAD and called for negotiations on the abolition of nuclear weapons, a position advocated by Niebuhr decades earlier.

Unlike Niebuhr, Walter Lippmann rejected the view that the Soviet Union was driven by ideology. He considered a "containment" policy a "strategic monstrosity" that would cause the United States to align itself with dubious puppet regimes and stretch its military resources to every corner of the globe. Instead, Lippmann suggested that the United States attempt to dispel Soviet fears by proposing a mutual withdrawal of Soviet and American troops from Germany to demilitarize the Cold War. In 1917 Lippmann had helped draft Woodrow Wilson's famous Fourteen Points, which attempted to redraw the map of Europe around the principles of collective security and national self-determination. Given a second chance to consider how to remake Europe after World War II, Lippmann abandoned Wilsonian idealism. The eminent journalist concluded that the Soviet Union's behavior was consistent with Russia's czarist ambitions going back to Peter the Great and that its influence over eastern Europe was dictated by its national interests and security needs.

George Kennan, who died in 2005 at the age of 101, came closest in predicting how the Cold War would end—and he lived to see it. Kennan believed a US-USSR superpower confrontation could not continue indefinitely lest it result in the sort of nuclear holocaust that President Reagan once characterized as "Armageddon." Arguing that the communist political system was too irrational and repressive to last, he anticipated that the Soviet Union would eventually collapse.

As an American diplomat in Moscow and other foreign capitals in the 1930s and 1940s, Kennan was able to observe Soviet behavior from the Stalin purges of the mid-1930s to the breakup of the US-Soviet alliance at the end of the war. In an eight-thousand-word telegram sent to Washington from Moscow in February 1946, he concluded that "basic inner Russian necessities which existed before the recent war and exist today" were shaping Soviet foreign policies. Russian national insecurities and Marxist revolutionary ideology had created a fear of "capitalist encirclement" that the United States could not allay, and it was driving Soviet leaders to overthrow their foreign enemies and purge their internal ones. Kennan's so-called "long telegram" (later expanded into a famous 1947 essay in *Foreign Affairs* that was anonymously attributed to "X") recommended that Washington policymakers use all means short of war to contain Soviet expansion and wait for "the gradual mellowing of Soviet power."

Niebuhr served as an advisor to a Kennan-led policy planning group in 1948, but he had little influence over the experienced State Department official, who preferred Gibbon's *Decline and Fall of the Roman Empire* to Scripture in explaining the sources of Soviet behavior. While Niebuhr argued that Marxism was a secular version of religious redemption, Kennan dismissed it as "a fig leaf of moral and intellectual respectability" concealing Russia's historic insecurities. Kennan urged the United States to forgo efforts at postwar collaboration and predicted the eventual emergence of what would be called "détente." He objected when the Truman administration twisted his understanding of containment into a military doctrine and applied it to Asia and other parts of the world.

Morgenthau, Lippmann, and Kennan would change their prescriptions as historical developments outran their theoretical formulations, but none believed their ideas should apply to Asia, where nationalism and anticolonialism were at odds with Soviet imperialism. With the exception of Dean Acheson, Truman's secretary of state, the major foreign policy realists all turned against the Vietnam War. Niebuhr criticized Lyndon Johnson for pursuing a phantom democracy in the Mekong Delta, recalling the biblical warning "The beginning of all sin is pride." Pride takes over, Augustine taught, when a leader is "too pleased with himself." Rather than acknowledge a mistake, he seeks praise and "exaltation," which "abases the mind."[28]

In his final years, Niebuhr agonized over the arms race. He had defended America's nuclear buildup in the 1950s, arguing that opponents of nuclear arms were falling for a pacifism that would appease the Soviet Union, and in *The Irony of American History* (1952) he went so far as to accept the possibility of a nuclear confrontation: there would be no return to innocence, no escape from evil. But the two-term Eisenhower presidency compelled Niebuhr to reconsider his views. When Red Army tanks moved into Hungary to crush an anticommunist uprising in 1956, it was clear that the Soviets had called Secretary Dulles's bluff. The threat of massive retaliation, which implied an American nuclear response to an act of Soviet aggression, was either hollow or insane.

Convinced that survival was preferable to annihilation, Niebuhr began to consider the possibilities of peaceful coexistence. For a time he welcomed Henry Kissinger's *Nuclear Weapons and Foreign Policy* (1957), seeing it as a repudiation of the doctrine of massive retaliation, only to discover that its author had in mind not a strategy of limited war but further reliance on weapons of mass destruction. Henceforth, Niebuhr rejected nuclear stockpiling, believing that policymakers should aim to avoid war, not calculate the chances of surviving it. By the time John F. Kennedy entered the White House in 1961, the idea of a winnable nuclear war had become a fixation of the far Right, but it chastened the views of Americans who had lived through the Berlin showdown between the superpowers in 1961 and the Cuban missile crisis the following year.

Niebuhr turned his thought to Thomas Hobbes, the seventeenth-century thinker who taught that the highest aim of politics was the preservation of life, not the salvation of the soul. In a 1963 essay, "History's Limitation in the Nuclear Age," Niebuhr observed that the reality of technology required a reconsideration of theology: "Any effort to bring history to a victorious conclusion by a final assault upon 'evil' forces such as communism could bring our whole civilization to a sorry end."[29]

A quarter century later Ronald Reagan expressed similar sentiments for the same reasons. He believed the Soviet Union was an "evil empire," but he knew the weapons designed to destroy it in America's defense would destroy all life, rendering futile an attempt to escape the tragedy of history. Reagan knew the Cold War offered no morally good choices. He was shaken when he saw the explosion of the space shuttle *Challenger* in 1986 and moved to hear the atheist Mikhail Gorbachev say "God help us" after the nuclear disaster at Chernobyl the same year. The religious imagination is shadowed by the thought of catastrophe.[30] The tragic hero, Niebuhr taught, perishes not because he is weak but because he is strong, possessed of the proud delusion that evil can be annihilated and history redeemed.

4

The Opening of the American Mind

NIEBUHR'S SOCIAL THOUGHT: "MASOCHISM" OR "WISDOM"?

If Reinhold Niebuhr's Cold War attitudes foreshadowed Ronald Reagan's anxieties about nuclear warfare and his urge to abolish nuclear weapons, the same comparison cannot be made of their respective views on domestic policy. Though a critic of the liberal idealism of his fellow Protestants, Niebuhr endorsed the liberal policies of his fellow Democrats, calling for government policies that would be anathema to most conservatives today. In the 1930s Niebuhr had taken far more radical positions, condemning the capitalist system and even suggesting that exploited workers might be forced to resort to violence to obtain justice. But a grudging and gradual appreciation for Roosevelt's New Deal and strong support for US intervention to aid Great Britain at the start of World War II pushed him toward the liberal political outlook he would retain for the rest of his life.

It would seem remarkable today for a theologian to command attention from both liberal thinkers and America's popular press, but the crisis atmosphere of the war years and the Cold War opened ears to Niebuhr's stern and prophetic warnings against the dangers of pride and the power of evil. How could citizens square their hopes for a better world with the reality of totalitarianism, the revelation of the Holocaust, and the inescapability of nuclear weapons? Did Niebuhr's religion offer an answer?

Not everyone was persuaded that it did. Leftist intellectuals were always baffled by Niebuhr's discourses on evil and sin. Taught by Marx that men and women are "species beings," born with natural needs for the body but not the alienated desires of an acquisitive society, they were at a loss to explain the theologian's belief in humankind's "fallen" nature. The socialist Irving Howe observed that sin "is a category of political moralists, not of psychologists and anthropologists, who in fact have marshaled considerable evidence to show that in some societies (particularly among savages who have read neither Kierkegaard nor Niebuhr) it does not exist."[1] The idea that alienation and exploitation persist in a broken world, with or without capitalism, was inadmissible to the Left.

More telling critiques of Niebuhr came from fellow theologians. They wondered on what basis he proclaimed humankind inexorably fated to sin but inexplicably obliged to resist temptation. Rabbi Abraham Heschel agreed with Niebuhr on the "ambiguity of virtue": pride and temptation color even good deeds. But Heschel warned that biblical history does not teach the inevitability of vanity and corruption as much as the need to purify desire by knowing God's will. The Jesuit Gustave Weigel commended Niebuhr's intelligence and learning, but observed that because Niebuhr accepted neither an infallible church nor an inerrant Scripture "Niebuhrian theology is ultimately an affirmation of the absoluteness of the unknown God beyond history, with a thoroughgoing relativism for everything in history." Weigel chided, "A Catholic with gentle malice might ask Niebuhr if his transcendental principle of relativism is *absolutely* valid."[2]

In liberal circles, salvos against Niebuhr's increasing influence were launched by Charles Frankel in *The Case for Modern Man* (1955) and Morton White, who focused his 1957 epilogue to *Social Thought in America: The Revolt against Formalism* (1949) on Niebuhr and Walter Lippmann. Frankel and White were trained philosophers of pragmatic bent who thought the idea of sin should be shelved along with histories of the Middle Ages. Both held that what can be known depends on what can be experienced, and they rejected explanations of natural events requiring supernatural, metaphysical, or subjectivist reasoning.

Frankel's text criticized Niebuhr and other contemporary thinkers who cast doubt on reason's capacity to improve human affairs, an outlook that Frankel was pleased to call Liberalism. Frankel compared a diverse group of writers who were skeptical about the outcome of scientific knowledge and social progress. Some (the Thomist Jacques Maritain) sought authoritative knowledge in eternal truths, while others (the sociologist Karl Mannheim) were sure that all knowledge was limited and partial, determined by social context and historical conditions. Still others (the British historian Arnold Toynbee in his ten-volume *A Study of History* [1929-1954]) attributed to seers, saints, and mystics the "transfiguration" of civilizations that respond creatively to challenge. "With Mr. Niebuhr," wrote Frankel, Toynbee "affirms the ubiquity of original sin; but he goes beyond Mr. Niebuhr and sets as the goal of all history the ultimate elimination of original sin."

Frankel was disturbed by what he considered "intellectual obscurity" masquerading as higher wisdom, and "cosmic hypochondria . . . which makes anguish and sin, mystery and frustration, the plan of the universe and the keys to history." He worried that a "negative and defensive" attitude was growing in liberals, who no longer seemed able to imagine progress and a better society. While agreeing with Niebuhr that liberalism's optimistic view of human nature ill prepared it for the horrors of modern history, Frankel dissented from the view that a disillusioned idealism was the liberal's lot in life and that anxiety was the evidence of humanity's essential alienation. Anxiety, he countered boldly, was "the essential condition of intellectual and artistic creation, personal nobility, self-sacrifice, and everything that is finest in human history." Moreover, when Niebuhr insisted that the "taint of sin is present even in our benevolent actions" he obliterated the distinction between good and bad motives. "What genuine guidance can such a doctrine give us?" asked Frankel, who was certain that Niebuhrian liberalism was a theoretical cul-de-sac. Niebuhr's call to strive after an "impossible victory" while preparing to suffer an "inevitable defeat"—that was a formula for failure as well as frustration. "This is masochism, not wisdom."[3]

White's *Social Thought in America* offered a sympathetic analysis of major liberal thinkers whose most important work had appeared in the first decades of the twentieth century. Oliver Wendell Holmes Jr., Thorstein Veblen, Vernon Parrington, John Dewey, and Charles Beard were men who broke with the static categories of nineteenth-century thought, exposed the misuses of power and influence, and affirmed the capacity of reform ideas to adapt social institutions to changing circumstances. In a 1957 epilogue White contrasted his galaxy of secular heroes to Niebuhr and to Lippmann, whose most recent book had argued that the teachings of natural law would curb the popular passions that give rise to tyranny. How was it conceivable that such ideas as original sin and natural law, fit for crumbling cathedrals, could achieve prominence? "It seems to me a sad commentary on the social thought of today," White concluded, "that two of the most popular social thinkers on the American scene can produce nothing more original or natural than the doctrines of original sin and natural law as answers to the pressing problems of this age."[4]

Niebuhr was upset to be grouped with Lippmann, who began to explore Thomist theology before the start of World War II but did not publish *Essays in the Public Philosophy* until 1955 (by which time its author doubted that Americans would submit to natural law or anything else that infringed on their rights). Niebuhr considered his Protestant existentialism a far cry from the journalist's Catholic essentialism, which turned paradoxes into platitudes.

White's epilogue was as much a spirited defense of Dewey and pragmatism as a critique of Niebuhr and sin. While he conceded that Dewey too often engaged in "cheer-leading" for science and its "methodolatry," White faulted Niebuhr for asserting that Dewey naively believed intelligence could replace war in human affairs. In truth, Dewey had once claimed that political leaders could use reason to shape war's outcome; that was his argument for supporting America's entry into World War I in 1917. But in 1939 Dewey repudiated that view, urging America to stay out of Europe's wars and arguing that the right response to Nazi aggression was reason, intelligence, and negotiation. White did not see fit to comment on Dewey's political bad judgment. When pragmatism's champion put his philosophy into practice—the basis on which it asks to be judged—he reached all the wrong conclusions. Instead, White emphasized the contradiction in Niebuhr's contention that moral action is necessary even though evil is unavoidable, the basis for the theologian's claim that man is both the creator and creature of history.

Both Frankel and White believed Niebuhr's theology was inadequate to address the immense issues facing America at home and abroad. Scientific method applied to practical problems might bring order out of chaos, but religion, which pondered the unknowable, was no place to deal with the "pressing problems of this age."[5] Yet a look at how Niebuhr addressed some of the social issues of his day gives us reason to question their dismissive attitude toward religion. The theologian always began with an understanding of power. Without the corrective of religion, power would always overcome the "children of light." Power was as inevitable as sin; it was will without conscience. But it was also not alien to freedom, for humankind both loved power and used it. Niebuhr, who once regarded power as an instrument of immoral society, would qualify his doctrine of power in the 1940s. In the right hands, used for the right reasons, it could become a force for social justice.

THE RIGHTS OF LABOR, THE CAUSE OF WOMEN, THE CASE FOR ZIONISM

When Niebuhr explained the significance of original sin many Americans inaccurately concluded that his "conservative" theology must give rise to a conservative politics. Did not unremitting sin render one's own capacities suspect and require submission to authority? On the contrary, Niebuhr held that the freedom of humankind demanded the pursuit of justice to mitigate the effects of sin. Among the victims of sin were those who labored. In classical and Christian thought, labor had neither status nor value. Labor was the burden of slavery and the punishment for disobedience to God. Not until John Calvin did labor take on dignity in God's eyes and not until John Locke did it secure human rights and liberties through the institution of property. For Karl Marx labor became so redemptive that Niebuhr considered communism a false religion promising the end of estrangement and a classless society.

Niebuhr advocated social justice for workers from the moment he came of political age during World War I. He supported factory laborers and settlement workers as a preacher in Detroit, and he lent his name and voice to the Socialist Party and its causes in the 1930s. He strongly supported passage of the Wagner Act of 1935, which gave unions the right to organize workers and bargain on their collective behalf, and he endorsed the merger of the AFL and CIO in 1955, arguing that in a democracy big business must be opposed by big labor to maintain a balance of power. In championing labor leaders such as Walter Reuther and rising labor-backed politicians such as Minneapolis mayor Hubert Humphrey, Niebuhr aimed to weaken the appeal of both left-wing communism and right-wing individualism. While he recognized that organized labor could be corrupted, Niebuhr opposed "right to work" laws prohibiting compulsory union membership, asserting that calls to protect "individual liberties" in a mass society preserved corporate collusion, not competitive capitalism.

Niebuhr realized that power acts in concert, and that the most effective strategy to oppose it is with countervailing power, an argument that hearkened back to *Moral Man and Immoral Society*. That book contained many references to Marxism, whose ideas were as wrong as its appeal was palpable. But Niebuhr's hero was not Marx but Lincoln, the Calvinist president who said, "Capital is only the fruit of labor, and could never have existed if labor had not first existed."[6]

Lincoln knew that the outcome of history vindicated no group. The president who wrote that both North and South "read the same Bible and pray to the same God" was sure that "the Almighty has his own purposes" and that they were unknowable. But despite what he called "the element of pretense in the idealism of both sides," Niebuhr believed God's purposes were not unrelated to human-kind's pursuit of justice. Niebuhr quoted Lincoln on slavery:

> Slavery was to be condemned even if it claimed divine sanction, for: "It may seem strange that any men should dare to ask a just God's assistance in wringing their bread from the sweat of other men's faces."[7]

Nicbuhr believed workers had rights that were trampled on by Marxist claims to end worker exploitation through revolution and collectivism. But the rights of labor also exceeded the rights that capitalists invoked to secure private property and uphold individualism. "Both creeds miss the truth about property," Niebuhr wrote in *The Irony of American History*, his great meditation on the character of the American nation. "Since property is a form of power, it cannot be unambiguously a source of social peace and justice."[8]

Women's struggle for justice raised similar issues of means and ends. In Niebuhr's writings on social ethics and justice in the 1920s there are relatively few references to women. However, in *Moral Man and Immoral Society* Niebuhr considered how men used their power over women to establish a claim to dominion. For women to overcome these claims moral arguments would not suffice. Niebuhr observed that women were unable to introduce "the principle of mutuality" into family life until they acquired economic power, which first required them to secure political power in the struggle over suffrage.[9]

There is nothing in Niebuhr's work to suggest that he would have agreed with the modern poststructuralist claim that women's nature is a social construction. "The purpose of history, guided by genealogy," wrote Michel Foucault, "is not to discover the roots of our identity but to commit itself to its dissipation."[10] Niebuhr, how-ever, held that humankind's fallen nature was real, and hence the feminist struggle was more than a political quest to overturn the oppressive norms of society; it was an element in a perilous aspiration to defy nature and assert human freedom:

> From the standpoint of certain rational and spiritual aspirations of the human spirit the differences between the sexes are irrational and illogical. Biological facts have determined motherhood to be a more absorbing vocation than the avocation of fatherhood, and thereby inhibited a mother's freedom in developing certain talents which are irrelevant to the maternal function. An adequate social morality will neither exclude women from the professions because of this fact, nor yet quarrel with nature to the extent of imperiling the responsibilities of motherhood.[11]

While women's rights are rightfully won in defiance of biological nature, Niebuhr suggested that it was a mistake to ignore the tasks of motherhood that separate women from men: "The truth in modern feminism came into history with some help from the errors of an inorganic and libertarian conception of the family and of an abstract rationalism which defied the facts of nature." On the other hand, he admitted that the tasks of motherhood become a convenient rationalization men use to assert the will to power.

> It must be added that the wisdom of the past which recognized the hazard to family life in the freedom of women, was not devoid of the taint of male "ideology." The male oligarchy used fixed principles of natural law to preserve its privileges and powers against a new emergent in history.[12]

Some feminists have argued that women's struggles are undermined by Niebuhr's preoccupation with sin, which regards every assertion of human rights as a possible occasion for the expression of pride and the will to power. They also suspect his concept of love, which entails a renunciation of self-interest. Yet Niebuhr never denied the dignity and self-respect due both women and men in all stations of life. What he warned against was self-deceit, the tendency to confuse ego with conscience, self-interest with idealism, and the collective interest of the group and nation with the good of humanity.

In one respect Niebuhr anticipated later poststructuralists when he proposed a historicist explanation for the origins of the family. The family is "so obviously the most primordial of human communities," he explained In *Man's Nature and His Communities* (1965), that it is considered "the 'natural' base" for all social customs and institutions. He argued, however, that the family "is itself a historical product" to the extent that humankind is free and a creator of its own history. Niebuhr criticized Aristotle's "erroneous analogy between animal and human communities" which stipulated that the family must be part of the natural order because sex is necessary for procreation. It was not the sexual partnership of male and female that created the institution of the family, Niebuhr averred, but the prolonged dependence of children on the mother, "who is the more obvious parent of the offspring." The family was thus a social product, something formed over time, not based in nature:

> Every extension of community in history embodies some contrivance of priest, soldier, or statecraft, designed to extend, circumvent or suppress a more "natural" form of cohesion.

Likewise, Niebuhr noted that patriarchy is an artifice of history:

> Aristotle commits the familiar error of regarding the dominion of the father as primordial, when probably matriarchy preceded male dominion in actual history for the obvious reason that the mother's relation to the offspring was more patent and potent in primitive communities than that of the father.

Niebuhr's questioning of the origins of paternal authority was rather like that of Henry Adams, who had argued in his brilliant and provocative essay "The Primitive Rights of Women" that the earliest family relationships and responsibilities depended upon the consent of women. Niebuhr appealed to Homer and other sources for evidence of the dominant role of women in ancient society:

> Paternal authority, even more than the family itself, was not only a historical development but a comparatively late one. Even before the age of the philosophers, the Greek dramatists portrayed themes in which the echoes of a previous struggle between the original matriarchal and the emerging patriarchal forms of family authority were reflected.

Aristotle's errors extended to the polis, the civil community in ancient Greece, which the philosopher ascribed to a rationally conceived constitution made possible by a social instinct "implanted in all men by nature." Plato made the analogy explicit with his depiction of a philosopher-king ruling society as reason rules the self. Yet in idealizing an aristocratic social structure neither philosopher would admit what the historian Thucydides rightly understood and vividly described: Ancient Greece concealed a will to power that was tearing it apart. Perhaps a Freud or a Marx could begin to analyze the rationalizations and ideologies used to justify a civilization's sexual roles and social forms. But Niebuhr held that Christian realism best appreciated the ways self-regard wars with self-transcendence, using power to corrupt motives in sex as in society.[13]

Niebuhr had no prejudices about woman's place. He rejected the notion that sacrificial love was a uniquely feminine trait and he supported women's professional aspirations. He did not believe sex was sinful but, like the other deadly sins, thought it could become the occasion for self-love or "an effort to escape the prison house of self by finding a god in a process or person outside the self."[14] Niebuhr was upset by the publication of the Kinsey Reports on male and female sexual behavior (1948, 1953), with their celebratory treatment of private lust as a public statistic, and he was troubled by the second wave of feminism that crested in the late 1960s, with its focus less on legal rights than on the assertion of new social and sexual roles. But perhaps that had less to do with his ideas than with his energetically public-spirited and upright personality. His friend and colleague Paul Tillich, who shared something of Niebuhr's neo-orthodox theological background, welcomed the signs of sexual liberation in America. Tillich, however, who came to Union Theological Seminary by way of Weimar Berlin, had an open marriage and a swinging lifestyle.[15]

Niebuhr lived to see the sixties generation put religion on trial. The Dionysian counterculture had little interest in either early Christianity—whose asceticism freed the spirit from the self-loathing of bodily pleasure—or ancient classical thought, which aspired to a wisdom that comes to those past the carnal impulses of youth. If the sixties generation refused to trust anyone over thirty, it did trust whatever would release the mind from guilt and fulfill the desires of the flesh. It may have reminded Niebuhr of Saint Augustine, whose longing for renunciation led him to implore God: "Give me chastity and continence, but not yet." In book 8 of his *Confessions*, the great saint admitted that he would rather see the sensual desires of youth "satisfied" than "extinguished."

Niebuhr welcomed Sigmund Freud's criticisms of liberal idealism and his efforts to understand the divided self, but he regarded Freudianism as another form of deterministic naturalism. What Marxism was to proletarians, Freudianism was to the upper middle class, "a typical product of the uneasy conscience . . . which has discovered the realm of chaos under the pretenses and partial achievements of rational order and discipline."[16] The Freudian superego was no substitute for a conscience. Niebuhr was dismissive toward writers such as Erich Fromm, who proposed to overcome personal and social repression and free the mind of anxiety and guilt. Instead of encouraging self-realization, Niebuhr thought what the self required was "an object of devotion beyond itself." Still, it's worth noting that Niebuhr visited the psychoanalyst Erik Erikson for help with crippling bouts of depression he suffered after a debilitating stroke in 1952.[17]

• • •

Niebuhr was far less troubled over the sexual and social relations of men and women than he was over the events of modern history, which inflicted far greater cruelties. For most students of history the twentieth century seemed to dash the optimism of nineteenth-century Western civilization. A Cold War that threatened nuclear annihilation was preceded by two world wars, an economic depression, the rise of totalitarian ideologies and the horror of the Holocaust, which occurred as governments and churches looked the other way rather than face up to the reality of radical evil.

Niebuhr never forgot the fate of Dietrich Bonhoeffer, the German theologian who became an outspoken defender of the victims of Nazi tyranny and the rights of the Christian church. Young Bonhoeffer spent a year in residence at Union Theological Seminary in 1930 and returned in 1939 to a faculty position Niebuhr helped him secure. But the safety of New York burdened his conscience, and after little more than a month he returned to Germany against the warnings of mentors and friends. He later joined the resistance and, praying for Germany's defeat, forsook his pacifist views and took part in an attempt to assassinate Hitler. Bonhoeffer was arrested in 1943 and executed in April 1945, shortly before the Allies liberated his camp. A martyr and moral exemplar, Bonhoeffer taught that ethics is derived not from the lessons one draws from religious texts but from the decisions one makes in the trials of life.

The horror of fascism is not only that it was perpetrated by moral monsters but that few voices of authority called for resistance to the atrocities of the Black Shirts and Brown Shirts. In Rome in 1943, the Nazis rounded up and deported Italian Jews under the windows of the Vatican. Some Catholic parish priests courageously hid Jews and helped them escape, but the Roman Catholic Church, an institution that teaches obedience to authority, was unwilling to protest the Nazi treatment of the Jews.

Enlightened and secular elites also failed the Jews. Hannah Arendt famously traced the political causes of anti-Semitism in *The Origins of Totalitarianism* (1951). She described how enlightened Europe assimilated prosperous Jews but failed to protect them from social discrimination, and her account of liberalism's indifference to the religion of the Jews echoed Niebuhr's view of the children of light. Secular and Christian liberals expected Europe's Jews to embrace pluralistic democracy, but this, wrote Niebuhr, was nothing more than a "provisional tolerance." Liberals were hard pressed to credit Jews' insistence on their religious and ethnic identity. But prejudice against Jews was prompted by their identity, which "stubbornly resists assimilation, both ethnically and religiously." Niebuhr urged recognition of Jewish particularity: Christians should stop trying to convert Jews, and liberals should stop trying to assimilate them.

Niebuhr had long admired Jews, whose "superiority in civic virtue" seemed to him the cause of their sympathy for the poor and the powerless. He noted that "they have the same superiority of other minority groups, including women." He respected the excellence of Jewish scholarship, particularly the work of Martin Buber, and the social conscience of leaders like Rabbi Stephen Wise. Arguably, Niebuhr's leading disciple was Will Herberg, once a Marxist ideologue, whose efforts to understand the nature and uses of power led him to the ideas of Niebuhr, Buber, Kierkegaard, and the tortured Russian Nicholas Berdyaev. It was Niebuhr who convinced Herberg to pursue the development of a Jewish theology rather than to convert to Christianity.[18]

The problem for Jews was not who they were but where they would live. During the war Niebuhr supported organizations to rescue Jewish and antifascist refugees. He later worked with the American Christian Palestine Committee to promote the Zionist cause, even though he knew a Jewish homeland would dispossess Arab Palestinians. In a two-part 1942 essay, "Jews after the War," Niebuhr instructed liberals that they must stop thinking that their task was simply to reabsorb displaced Jews into a new Europe purged of race bigotry and dedicated to the universal principles of democracy, tolerance and pluralism. That view was not only historically naive with regard to European anti-Semitism but was based on the sort of shallow Enlightenment liberalism that misunderstood the nature of the self. The liberalism needed was not one preoccupied by an ideology of personal rights but one focused on an oppressed people's collective claim to security in a dangerous world of competing powers. Its goal for Jews was "a homeland in which they will not be simply tolerated but which they will possess."[19]

When the Truman administration accepted the United Nations plan for the partition of Palestine in 1947, few Western writers could anticipate the impossible solution it created after Israel declared statehood the following year. "For the Jews in Palestine," writes David Remnick, "Zionism was a movement for national liberation after untold suffering; for the Arabs, Zionism was an intolerable assault by the colonial West against sacred grounds and Islam itself."[20] Niebuhr, who focused his thinking on Christians and Jews, gave almost no thought to Islam and the Arabs. Indeed, he implied that the Middle East was a relic of the past without a future.

CIVIL RIGHTS AND MARTIN LUTHER KING JR.

What future did Reinhold Niebuhr envision for African Americans? Biographer Richard Fox judged the theologian to have been slow to respond to the problems of racism in America. He noted that Niebuhr served on panels and prepared reports calling for better educational and economic opportunities for blacks, but that he neglected to explain that racism was responsible for the absence of opportunity. Fox suggested that Niebuhr's "Christian prophecy was so completely rooted in his reading of the industrial conflict between skilled white workers and their employers" that he marginalized the importance of African American participation in the political process.[21] Like Jews in Christian America, blacks were a minority in a democracy that always favored the majority's choices. The theologian would need Tocqueville's wisdom to understand that democratic society is as much a problem as a solution when racial minority groups seek a redress of grievances.

Niebuhr also needed the greater moral urgency of a Martin Luther King Jr. to compel the majority to recognize the minority's rights. For King the civil rights movement was a struggle for freedom, not democracy. King realized that blacks would need the authority of the courts to interpret the Constitution, the law of the land, and that they would need the power of government to enforce the courts' decisions. Hence the struggle for freedom was inseparable from the exercise of power. A racial minority bent on self-determination needed state power to deliver it from oppression. But where in a democracy was one to find power when it was lodged in the consent of a majority that refused to extend it to black Americans? Once again American liberalism had to face up to its own paradoxes.

Niebuhr could hardly agree with progressive intellectuals who believed that the answer was for education to dispel ignorance and bigotry, paving the way for democracy to enact racial equality. But neither was he convinced that the Supreme Court's authority was sufficient to end segregation and change public attitudes on race relations. Niebuhr's critics have taken note of his cautious response to the US Supreme Court's 1954 decision in *Brown v. Board of Education*, which overturned the "separate but equal" doctrine that allowed states to maintain school segregation. Niebuhr said political and social change would need to be gradual to be effective, and he agreed with liberals such as Eleanor Roosevelt and Adlai Stevenson that judicial fiat alone could not overcome the attitudes of the white South. Once he even turned down Martin Luther King's request that he sign a petition urging President Eisenhower to intervene to prevent the outbreak of white violence.[22]

Such caution was not uncommon in the 1950s. Indeed, after Eisenhower sent troops to Little Rock, Arkansas, in 1957 to desegregate its public schools, Hannah Arendt wrote a controversial and much discussed essay, "Reflections on Little Rock," criticizing his decision and arguing that while democracy is the province of politics, discrimination is the prerogative of society. She cited the novelist William Faulkner's pronouncement that enforced integration was no better than enforced segregation.[23] For Arendt to oppose the course of the civil rights movement may represent a lamentable lapse in judgment, but it was an outgrowth of her political philosophy, which recognized boundaries separating citizen rights from social freedoms.

By reversing the flow of power the civil rights movement invalidated the claims of some groups and legitimized those of others:

Black and white "freedom riders" ended white Southerners' freedom to discriminate and protected black Southerners' freedom from discrimination. King's political strategy of nonviolent direct action made front page headlines, and the marches and demonstrations he led became a staple of the evening television news. But while many Americans were moved by King's eloquent "I Have a Dream" speech on the steps of the Lincoln Memorial, they were angered when civil rights protesters blocked city streets and staged sit-ins and boycotts to force public officials to change the law. King always insisted that the movement's nonviolent tactics were aimed at the conscience of whites. In this sense, King was a religious idealist. But King was also a student of Niebuhr's theology—he wrote two essays on Niebuhr in seminary—and he understood that power is necessary to achieve justice in the city of man.

In "A Letter from a Birmingham Jail" and in other addresses, King drew on Augustine and Aquinas to teach that those who seek justice have a responsibility to disobey unjust laws. He referred to Buber to explain why genuine human relationships connect "I" to "Thou," and he cited Tillich to preach that sin is separation. But when he discussed the uses of power, King drew upon Niebuhr, explaining that those who have power seldom relinquish it without a struggle, and that those who would make moral claims to their civil rights must acquire the power to attain them. King believed civil disobedience was consistent with a philosophy of nonviolence, but his advocacy of specific "direct action" tactics—demonstrations, strikes, boycotts, sit-ins—reflected a Niebuhrian understanding that the strategic application of force must be brought to bear on situations unresponsive to reason and religion, resistant to the arguments of mind and appeals to the heart.

And yet power itself remains a source of corruption. If the fear of racial backlash made Niebuhr hesitate to use federal power in the 1950s, the subsequent rise of "black power" stirred as much uneasiness in him as it did in other New York intellectuals, from Norman Mailer, whose "The White Negro" (1957) anxiously observed the rise of a black-influenced "hip" culture intimidating the "squares," to Norman Podhoretz, whose "My Negro Problem—and Yours" (1963) pondered white fears of black fearlessness. Much to the dismay of academic liberals, the Black Panthers, with their leather jackets and Maoist pamphlets proclaiming that power grows from the barrel of a gun, were lionized on many college campuses.

Niebuhr died in 1971, three years after the assassination of Martin Luther King Jr. By this time the moral force of the civil rights movement had either dissolved into black rage or refocused its energy on court cases rather than street demonstrations. Niebuhr, who regretted that ill health had kept him from joining King on the civil rights march from Selma to Montgomery in 1965, praised King as "the most creative Protestant, white or black."[24] King was more realistic and courageous than the militant radicals who tried in vain to tear down the system without understanding how power works to preserve it. He understood that the cause of civil rights was a moral crusade to redeem America so that white Americans would recognize the humanity of black Americans.

Yet Niebuhr had to face his own dilemmas. Doing justice to black Americans ultimately depended on the authority of a legal system rather than on the prophecy of a preacher or the moral convictions of a people. This not only diluted black idealism but complicated the work of religion. Niebuhr defended the cause of civil rights as the just politics of an embattled and beleaguered group. Like the labor movement and the cause of women, the civil rights movement was focused on social injustices; it had real grievances and represented legitimate concerns that had to be addressed. However, Niebuhr doubted that civil society could ever rely on the moral impulses of the self to extend justice to others. Christianity admonishes humankind to love thy neighbor as thyself, but Niebuhr questioned the capacity of love to secure justice:

> Actually both admonitions, that the self ought to love itself and that the self ought to love others, are spiritually impotent. An insecure impoverished self is not made more secure by the admonition to be concerned for itself; for an excessive concern for its insecurity is the cause of its impoverishment. Nor is it made secure by the admonition to love others because that is precisely what it cannot do

because of its anxiety about itself. That is why a profound religion has always insisted that the self cannot be cured by law but only by grace; and also why the profoundest forms of Christian faith regard this preoccupation as not fully curable and therefore as requiring another kind of grace: that of forgiveness.[25]

On many occasions King acknowledged his debt to Niebuhr for teaching him about the tenacity and temptations of power. But King also believed in the power of God's love to inspire brotherhood. Preaching to striking sanitation workers in Memphis on the evening before he was assassinated, King's words were apocalyptic. He enthralled his listeners by telling them the tactics of nonviolence would prevail just as they had in Birmingham against the fire hoses and police dogs of Bull Connor. He told the story of the Good Samaritan "who had the capacity to project the 'I' into the 'Thou,' and to be concerned about his brother," no matter what the danger. And he expressed his satisfaction that "we, as a people, will get to the promised land." King knew this was so, he said, "because I've been to the mountaintop. . . . Mine eyes have seen the glory of the coming of the Lord!"[26]

Niebuhr was an excellent public speaker, but it is unlikely that he could have said that. He believed that sin blinds humankind to its own pride, that the root of sin is unbelief, and that unbelief cannot be overcome without a perfect trust in God's love, which is almost always impossible to attain. Humankind, wracked by anxiety, is perilously caught between its freedom and its finitude.

5

The Cunning of
American History

What Niebuhr thought of human beings he also thought of America. Our study concludes by considering *The Irony of American History*, his famous commentary on a nation that wanted to believe it always did the right thing for the right reasons—and that it always would be rewarded for doing so.

The Irony of American History has sometimes been dismissed as a tract for its times and an apology for American power during the first years of the Cold War. Niebuhr, it is true, did not ask the nation to reject a destiny that had been thrust upon it by world events. America in the 1950s was a morally self-righteous nation that believed its survival rested on its possession of the atomic bomb and its willingness to use it even if this threatened the destruction of the world. But Niebuhr believed America's world leadership in the struggle against communism was based on its extraordinary economic prosperity and technological prowess, not its eagerness for power politics, and he feared American innocence more than American experience. He urged the nation to surrender its illusions of "winning" the Cold War, but to persevere with humility, patience, and self-restraint. The danger was that a militarily strong

America might confuse its "mastery of nature with the mastery of history":

> We might be tempted to bring the whole of modern history to a tragic conclusion by one final and mighty effort to overcome its frustrations. The political term for such an effort is "preventive war." It is not an immediate temptation; but it could become so in the next decade or two.[1]

A few years after the book's publication, Niebuhr would ask the makers of American foreign policy to reconsider the doctrine of nuclear deterrence and to explore with the Soviet Union the possibilities of mutual disarmament. Recalling the Marshall Plan's role in Europe's economic recovery, he questioned why policymakers would rather threaten massive retaliation than support foreign aid. Fear inspired one approach, hope the other.

In the 1950s American foreign policy generated a rich debate between realists and idealists, advocates of containment and proponents of a roll-back of Soviet power. But when Russia invaded Hungary in 1956, America was unable to craft either a viable diplomatic solution or a military response. The failure of both reason and power was a demonstration of Niebuhr's argument that American idealism would have to come to terms with the limits of its moral striving. Despite US nuclear superiority over the Soviet Union, the Eisenhower administration could do nothing more than refer the matter to the United Nations Security Council to justify its own inaction. Niebuhr condemned Russian repression in Hungary, but his views had less to do with a strategy of international relations than with his religious sensibility, which informed his assessment of foreign affairs and his reading of American history.

The Irony of American History is not a call to moral clarity but an acknowledgment of moral ambiguity. America was compelled to summon its own countervailing power to resist the communist will to power, which was rooted in a false theory of history. But Niebuhr warned that liberalism was subject to its own illusions, which caused Americans to disavow, misconstrue, or misuse the power they possessed. Sometimes disdainful of power as the enemy of freedom, at other times boastful that their power derived from their virtue, Americans were caught up in embarrassing contradictions that were a cause and a consequence of the nation's history.

In the study's first pages Niebuhr concisely defined the meanings of pathos, tragedy, and irony and their relevance to the country's predicament. Pathos, he noted, elicits pity; what is pathetic is suffering that is generated by "confusions in life for which no reason can be given, or guilt ascribed." Tragedy, by contrast, "elicits admiration as well as pity because it combines nobility with guilt," as when an individual sacrifices one high value for the sake of another. Niebuhr cited as an example of a tragic dilemma America's willingness to threaten nuclear war to preserve world peace. He urged Americans to acknowledge that this made the nation complicit in the "prospective guilt of the atomic bomb" and to take responsibility for their actions.

It was the concept of irony, however, that Niebuhr found most appropriate for an analysis of American civilization. He observed:

> the ironic situation is distinguished from a pathetic one by the fact that the person involved in it bears some responsibility for it. It is differentiated from tragedy by the fact that the responsibility is related to an unconscious weakness rather than a conscious resolution.[2]

The American past certainly contained many instances of pathos and tragedy, but Niebuhr thought America's liberal culture made it particularly susceptible to irony:

> Irony however prompts some laughter and a nod of comprehension beyond the laugh; for irony involves comic absurdities which cease to be altogether absurd when fully understood.[3]

Niebuhr recalled that "our Calvinist and our Jeffersonian ancestors" had launched America as an example to the world. Contrary to historians who depicted them as a study in contrasts, Niebuhr asserted that the colonials of Massachusetts and Virginia were both convinced that prosperity and virtue went hand in hand, and that their flourishing in the new nation was due to divine providence. He noted that Americans had not failed miserably in this conceited endeavor but had succeeded "more obviously than any other nation." The United States had not only acquired vast wealth but enormous world power. The irony was that while riches increased the nation's strength and magnified its self-righteous belief in its own virtue, America's influence over other countries was ensnaring it in unsought responsibilities and diminishing its self-control. "Our very success in this enterprise has hastened the exposure of its final limits."[4]

Niebuhr explained that man's Fall precluded the possibility of any ultimate triumph. Were Americans to lose sight of the limits to their knowledge and power, they would fall victim to the sins of vanity and cupidity. But if the nation could check its dreams of mastering destiny and act with restraint and humility, then it might yet use its power wisely to thwart communism, whose pretensions to idealism masked a more brutal and cynical will.

NIEBUHR AND THE CONSENSUS HISTORIANS

The Irony of American History was published at a time when scholars were reinterpreting the American past in ways that came to be known as "consensus history." While differing with one another in important respects, historians such as Richard Hofstadter, Daniel J. Boorstin, and Louis Hartz all reacted to the economic and class-based interpretations of history that had changed the minds of the 1930s generation, books such as Charles Beard's *Economic Interpretation of the Constitution* (1913) and Vernon Parrington's *Main Currents in American Thought* (1927). While Beard, Parrington, and other "progressive" historians rejected the fantasy of Marxist determinism, they still viewed American history as a story of conflicts between rich and poor, oppressors and oppressed. Indeed, their outlook was not unlike Niebuhr's view of society to the extent that they saw American history in terms of struggles between social groups contending for power and control. The progressive historians championed Jeffersonians over Federalists, Jacksonians over Whigs, and Democrats over Republicans in party politics, and preferred agrarians to industrialists and democrats to capitalists in society.

By contrast, the emerging consensus history suggested that Americans shared common desires rooted in common values that were surprisingly constant throughout the nation's history. Despite political battles, party realignments, and social upheavals there were certain areas of basic agreement. Richard Hofstadter's *The American Political Tradition* (1948) summarized the continuity of the American creed from the colonial period to the present:

> The sanctity of private property, the right of the individual to dispose of and invest it, the value of opportunity, and the natural evolution of self-interest and self-assertion, within broad legal limits, into a beneficent social order have been staple tenets of the central faith in American political ideology.[5]

Significantly, Hofstadter regarded self-interest as part of the "natural evolution" of the human species, agreeing with John Dewey, who believed it more likely that a "beneficent social order" could be achieved by understanding Darwin's theory of evolutionary struggle than by emulating Christ's ethic of self-sacrifice. What religion distrusted science legitimated.

The consensus historians gave scant attention to Niebuhr's argument from original sin, the view that conflict lies not in class or property but in the conceits and corruptions of human nature. Niebuhr warned against the pretensions to idealism that disguise self-interest, but in *The Genius of American Politics* (1953), the historian Daniel J. Boorstin celebrated just about everything Niebuhr lamented. Boorstin was pleased to report that what made America exceptional was its indifference to political philosophy, its complacent and unreflective acceptance of a celebratory "American way of life." The uniqueness of American history was its people's determined refusal to think about the values that should determine their actions and the principles that should form their politics. According to Boorstin, Americans drew their values from past political practices, legal precedents, and the lure of the land, attributes he called the "givenness" of experience, and not from anything so abstruse as theological puzzles and political theories that try to solve the mystery of mankind's inhumanity. Niebuhr wanted Americans to pay heed to a worried conscience struggling against the temptations of evil. Boorstin taught that there was nothing to worry about except worry itself.[6]

For Boorstin, the nation's "genius" was Americans' capacity to live within their country's political traditions, not to rethink them. A Communist Party member as a Harvard undergraduate, Boorstin warned Europeans against trying to save themselves from communism by replicating American "ideas" because "the remedy it seeks is itself a disease." Americans were fortunate to get along without developing explicit political ideas and values since theorizing only interfered with practical problem-solving.

Thus Boorstin extolled the Puritans for turning away from God and trusting in themselves. "From Providence to Pride" was the title of his chapter celebrating the disappearance of the Puritan mind from American history. While he admitted that Puritan writings were "works of rare seriousness and dignity," they represented efforts to "remold" the new continent according to theological precepts fit only for sustaining a tightly knit moral community. Succeeding generations of New Englanders had rightly moved "from a sense of mystery to a consciousness of mastery." Boorstin applauded the colonists' "growing tendency to make the 'is' the guide to the 'ought,' to make America as it was (or as they had now made it) a criterion of what America ought to be." The colonists became pragmatists who let their need to discover and conquer the natural environment set their moral agenda. As for religion in America, Boorstin contended that it was valued more for the social services it performed than for the truths it prophesied.[7]

Niebuhr agreed that the colonists had made the transition from mystery to mastery, transforming themselves from Puritans into Yankees. But one is struck that in his initial discussion of the Puritans he missed seeing how different his own theology was from theirs at the very beginnings of American history. When the New England Puritans heard John Winthrop preach his sermon "A Modell of Christian Charity" (1629), they learned that they must "walke toward one another in love and mercy," be "knitte together in this worke as one man," look upon their enemies with compassion and forgiveness, work diligently, and regard their prosperity as a consequence of their piety. Once, when Winthrop was charged with overstepping his ministerial prerogatives, he defended himself by reminding his judges that "liberty is sin" and that they were obliged to obey his authority.

Niebuhr would agree with Winthrop that freedom makes evil possible, but would he not reject Winthrop's invocation to "a Citty upon a hill" as but another example of misguided American idealism? Niebuhr's reading of Augustine and other Christian thinkers had convinced him that it was not possible for the Christian principle of love to perpetuate a moral society such as the Puritans tried to establish in Massachusetts. Puritanism might survive as a small, self-contained community, but in America the Puritan covenant began to erode within a single generation, and the Puritan poets were haunted by a sense of universal sin. Unlike Niebuhr, they could not imagine how to achieve justice in an immoral society:

> For what is *Beauty*, but a fading flower?
> Or what is *Pleasure*, but the Devils bait,
> Whereby he catcheth whom he would devour,
> And multitudes of Souls doth ruinate?
> . . . .
> And what are *Riches* to be doted on?
> Uncertain, fickle, and ensnaring things;
> They draw Mens Souls into Perdition,
> And when most needed, take them to their wings.[8]

The colonists would learn in time to dote on riches, and they would no more obey a New England magistrate than they would a British monarch. The United States of America was born in flight from authority, yet the irony was that in pursuing their own interests and desires, the American people—moralists working upon matter—insisted on seeing themselves as living for God and country. It has been said that hypocrisy is the tribute vice pays to virtue. Niebuhr's *The Irony of American History* is a systematic study of those habits of vanity and self-delusion that allow Americans to pursue their ambitions, innocent of their motives and indifferent to the moral consequences of their actions.

. . .

The consensus school of history produced what I have elsewhere called "a Marxist description without a Marxist solution."⁹ Consensus historians emphasized how economics, environment, and social structures explained the continuity of American liberalism. But while Boorstin downplayed ideas in politics, Louis Hartz's *The Liberal Tradition in America* (1955) argued for the pervasiveness of liberalism arising out of two interrelated but hitherto unnoticed factors: the absence of feudalism and the presence of "Lockeanism." The first meant that in America there was no entrenched aristocracy with a vested interest in inequality or reasons to cling to religious dogmas that justified authority, hierarchy, and obedience. The corollary importance of John Locke's philosophy meant Americans saw themselves as entrepreneurs and property owners possessed of natural rights to the products of their labor. There were neither peasants nor proletarians in America, and hence there could be no socialists.

Hartz made no mention of Niebuhr, but his text contains an irony that a Niebuhrian could appreciate. While religion was often identified with an authoritarian defense of the old order, in early America there was no old order. The American Revolution was the only modern revolution that had the church on its side, and members of all social groups joined the revolutionary cause, making it unlikely that America would experience the kind of cultural warfare that characterized political life in Europe.

Religion in America satisfied the self's need for well-being more than its hunger for the sacred or the sacrificial. Tocqueville had noted that Americans continually spoke of "self-interest properly understood" to show that being virtuous was compatible with calculating one's own advantage, even in matters of religion. Preachers in America, he wrote, "are forever pointing out how religious beliefs favor freedom and public order, and it is often difficult to be sure when listening to them whether the main object of religion is to procure eternal felicity in the next world or prosperity in this."[10] The Frenchman explained that by democratizing religion, making it a popular resource for social good, Americans were discarding the doctrines of sin and atonement. Liberalism in America enabled Americans to "be religious" without submitting to any demands, to seek Christ without the cross.

In their respective studies of American political philosophy, Niebuhr and Hartz described how Americans fooled themselves about their own goals and about how to achieve them. The most important American goal was to defend freedom, and the principal self-deception was the belief that the enemy of freedom is power.

Hartz described how in the eighteenth and early nineteenth centuries Jeffersonian and Jacksonian democrats denounced national banks and corporate charters as warrants for the exercise of "aristocratic" class privilege, and they resisted Federalist and Whig attempts to vest power in the federal government. Liberals in Europe had developed theories of national sovereignty and centralized power to justify the destruction of the hated *ancien regime*. But Americans had no need to destroy an aristocratic class or feudal laws, and so they professed to detest the authority of government. By resorting to checks and balances and the separation of powers, the Constitution almost qualified sovereignty out of existence. Hartz further noticed that Jeffersonians feared people in cities just as Hamiltonians feared "the masses." Each party failed to understand the alchemy of liberalism: "The mass of the people . . . are bound to be capitalistic, and capitalism, with its spirit disseminated widely, is bound to be democratic."[11]

There are further ironies: Once capitalists and industrialists abandoned their defensive hostility to democracy in the later nineteenth and twentieth centuries, they were able to turn the tables on the progressives, branding them as "un-American" and "social-ist" if they dared to suggest that government should exercise power to curtail privilege and expand rights. For their part, progressives like Beard and Parrington proceeded "to draw a red herring across the track of the American democrat's own liberal capitalist charac-ter." The progressive historians failed to see that private economic power increased with every expansion of government, and so they described each chapter in the nation's story as a titanic struggle be-tween "conservatives" and "radicals."

Seeing the state as a source of tyranny rather than a guarantor of liberty and security, Americans could hardly admit that their own desires and actions were responsible for the increase and concen-tration of government power. The federal government was typically portrayed in opposition to the people, the very government the people looked to for protection, services, and benefits. Americans rarely conceded their own hypocrisy. Hartz underscored the matter by pointing to "the rugged individualism of the American farmer." Protected by tariffs and subsidies, he "must surely fascinate any so-cial psychologist."[12]

Niebuhr's *The Irony of American History* strikingly foreshadows Hartz's *Liberal Tradition in America*, which was published three years later. One irony was that Americans were never as innocent as they pretended. The colonists believed they were pure of heart, having escaped an old world and created a new one. But this spiri-tual pride, Niebuhr noted, derived from the absence of class strug-gles and the abundance of economic opportunities, which served to "perpetuate Jeffersonian illusions about human nature."[13]

Like Hartz, Niebuhr found multiple ironies in American liber-alism—from the Jeffersonian democrats who feared the growth of government to the great capitalists who controlled the state while continually citing the Jeffersonian maxim that that government is best which governs least. Constant advances in scientific knowledge and industrial technology, along with a boundless frontier, nour-ished Americans' prideful conviction that prosperity came to all who were virtuous and virtue to all who were prosperous. Niebuhr further noted that the realities of power and self-interest were obscured by the idealism of classical liberalism, which claims that voluntarism is sufficient to bring about social harmony and that "the competition of interests will make for justice without political or moral regulation."[14]

Once the Depression exposed the failings of laissez-faire, the New Deal showed American democracy that it was possible to use political power to curb economic power. Yet America was continually tempted to bear false witness against itself, its vanity constantly on the hunt for flattery.

To write a moral history of the American republic the historian would need to explore what Americans refuse to know about themselves and explain the ways Americans deceive themselves. Niebuhr held that the study of history is no exercise in omniscience. Nothing supports either the ancients' cyclical views or the moderns' notions of progressive development, and Marxist and liberal idealists are mistaken to think they can discern the logic of history, its meaning, direction, and conclusion. But the history of men and women is not meaningless from the standpoint of religion. The end of history is not the culmination of events in time. It is a perspective on all of time. Niebuhr summed up what we could know about the "end" of history in one of his most beautiful passages:

> Nothing that is worth doing can be achieved in our lifetime; therefore we must be saved by hope. Nothing which is true or beautiful or good makes complete sense in any immediate context of history; therefore we must be saved by faith. Nothing we do, however virtuous, can be accomplished alone; therefore we are saved by love. No virtuous act is quite as virtuous from the standpoint of our friend or foe as it is from our standpoint. Therefore we must be saved by the final form of love which is forgiveness.[15]

A PHILOSOPHER OF HISTORY

Sometimes people think they know who they are and what they want and how to get it. But what if they are wrong about their identity, mistake their desires, and cannot govern their will? What if they are driven to act by forces alien to themselves? How then can they be considered free? And if their acts are not voluntary, can they be moral or immoral? Here difficulties arise for moral philosophy. Similarly, groups of people over periods of time often think they know what they want and why things happen and how they can influence the outcome of events. What if they are wrong? Are people the subjects of their own history, or are they its objects? What if events occur for reasons people do not recognize and cannot influence? These are matters for a philosophy of history.

At the moment when they first settled in Massachusetts Bay, the Puritan colonists believed that their intentions determined their personal salvation and their covenant between God and his people. Over time, however, they learned that their actions produced unintended consequences, the result of their desires but not the intended object of those desires. Niebuhr's good friend, the poet W. H. Auden, captured this quandary in a few lines:

> Some think they're strong, some think they're smart,
> Like butterflies they're pulled apart,
> America can break your heart.
> *You don't know all, sir, you don't know all.*[16]

Although Niebuhr never pretended to know all there is to know, America could still break his heart. Because the self is both a creator and creature of history, it can both shape history and be shaped by history to know itself as something other than itself. Niebuhr doubted the classical idea of self-mastery through reason, and he had no patience with the modern idea that the self is formed in relation to others, that identity is constructed in problem-solving and social interaction. In *The Self and the Dramas of History* (1955), Niebuhr recalled the great exchange between Erasmus and Luther. Erasmus extolled the freedom of the will that allows the self to control its impulses, while Luther explored the bondage of the will unable to resist the temptations of sin. Niebuhr wrestled with these perplexities, describing the conflict between freedom and determinism, the tension between human aspirations to freedom and love and the human achievements that are contingent and corrupt. Niebuhr held that America could not save the world and that history could not redeem humankind. As a philosopher of history he would refute these claims. He urged Americans to renounce the vanity of their idealism and to reject Marxist and liberal parables that final justice is discernable by reason and achievable by will.

Niebuhr bears comparison to the historian Henry Adams, who jested that his autobiography, *The Education of Henry Adams* (1918), was a continuation of *The Confessions of St. Augustine.* Augustine was the greater artist, wrote Adams, because his work began in "multiplicity" and ended in "unity," as God overcame the temptations of the flesh and resolved the chaos of the world. By contrast, Adams wrote, his account had to "reverse the method," as the forces governing life multiplied and accelerated, fragmenting knowledge, tormenting the mind, and leaving his story's final chapters "unmanageable."[17]

Niebuhr shared Adams's sense of irony but not his feelings of futility. He agreed with Augustine that the love of God is the essential ordering principle of the *civitas dei*. But he held that the conditions of the *civitas terrena* are set by the sinful self that remains a mystery to itself. The law of love is normative, but the fact of sin is universal. The self, even when it believes itself dedicated to a higher principle, may be caught up in self-love—a condition, said Niebuhr, that even the wise Augustine didn't quite understand.

In contemplating the wars of the twentieth century, Niebuhr followed a tradition that begins with Thucydides and reaches its literary flowering with Tolstoy, forming a company of those who reflect in sorrow on the chaos of history and stand in awe of the pitiless irrationality of war: Thucydides pondered the Peloponnesian War, Augustine the sack of Rome, Tolstoy the Napoleonic wars, Nietzsche the Franco-Prussian War, Arendt the Holocaust. None could come to terms with what Hegel called "the slaughter-bench of history."

In his second inaugural address, Abraham Lincoln said "the Almighty has His own purposes," unknown to humankind, for "the mighty scourge of war." But when human suffering and death become the stuff of history, then the question of history becomes the riddle of religion, and those who are religious question whether they are seeing the will of God or the actions of men.

The historian deals with the latter, explaining the ways of the self by giving an account of how men and women fulfill their needs and achieve their ambitions. Historians dismiss the soul as a mere figure of speech that represents the heart's desiring, not that which seeks to know the will of God and receive the assurance of forgiveness. Niebuhr, like Lincoln, could not explain the will of God, but the theologian would explain the ironies of a self that cannot know itself and a soul that cannot rule itself. When America became the object of the historian's inquiries, it lost its soul and found its self.[18]

6

God Is Dead—
Long Live Religion!

"Reinhold, we are all intrigued about your religious message. That is why I invited [J. B.] Priestley. We know all the modern stuff has broken down, but we don't think you can reconstruct the old and we would like to know how you do it."[1]

The theologian Reinhold Niebuhr listened to that curious interrogation by the British philosopher Martin Kinsley, which Niebuhr conveyed to his wife Ursula in a letter from London in 1943. Others who would wait for Niebuhr's explanation included Richard Crossman, Labour member of Parliament; R. H. Tawney, professor of economic history at the University of London and author of the influential *Religion and the Rise of Capitalism*; and W. H. Auden, the poet who saw Niebuhr as so restlessly inquisitive that he seemed "an ecclesiastical Orson Welles." American thinkers also questioned the tactics and intent of Niebuhr's effort to revive religion in an age of doubt and disbelief: the historian Arthur Schlesinger Jr., the diplomat George Kennan, and the young theology student Martin Luther King Jr. puzzled over the theologian's writings. In the letter to his wife, Niebuhr wrote not a word about how he might answer Kinsley's question. But the query itself should give us pause, for the theologian could well have replied: "God is dead—long live religion!"

Whether a supreme being exists was of less importance to Reinhold Niebuhr than the message Christianity holds out to humankind. The theologian would describe God as the center of meaning, the source of love, and "the ground of existence and the essence which transcends existence."[2] But these formulations were for him a "mythical paradox." Niebuhr treated as symbolic many of the claims made about God, which he took seriously but not literally. The biblical tale's depiction of the human condition had no need of historical verification. Neither was it possible or necessary to offer a reasoned conception of one's awareness of God, an assertion that upset Catholic theologians.[3] What was important was that humanity reflect on man's sin and God's grace, understand the persistence of human pride, and contemplate the mystery of divine transcendence. Niebuhr was intent on pondering the meaning of human history and the drama of the soul confronting freedom and fate, the promise of life and the inevitability of death.

Niebuhr felt God as more an absence than a presence, and he attempted to describe what God's absence meant for the self, which is the core of human existence. For Niebuhr the self is finite and in a state of constant anxiety, susceptible to self-seeking and self-deceit. Niebuhr's quarrel was not with God but with God's fallen creatures, especially men and women who refuse to face the limits of their own human nature and strut high and mighty through life, victims of pride and blind to sin.

• • •

Today America's political and business leaders typically announce that "freedom" is the touchstone of all their efforts, the benchmark against which we are to measure their accomplishments. The term is our national creed. Centuries ago freedom was considered a passion to be controlled; today it is a principle to be celebrated. Educators teach it, poets chant it, philosophers define it, moralists preach it, politicians swear by it, the retired enjoy it, immigrants dream of it, and the poor strive for it.

The cult of freedom is so ubiquitous in American history that it continually erodes the binding force of authority, a concept carrying weight mainly in Supreme Court rulings and the tenets of religious sects. Many Americans regard authority as inherently alien and illegitimate, and on this the extremes meet. For the far Right the federal government is a threat to liberty, while the radical Left views corporate capitalism as a threat to democracy. Significantly, both are influenced by European thought: the Austrian school of economics warns Americans against creeping socialism, the French-German school of postmodernism against incipient fascism. Still, Americans respond less to European fears than to their own native-born hopes, best expressed in Walt Whitman's "Resist much / Obey little."

Preoccupied with the fetish of freedom, few Americans dwell on its riddles and paradoxes. We readily assume that to be free is to do what we wish. But are not our wishes often subject to passions that affect our actions? Genuine freedom consists in self-mastery, escape from external restraints and inner compulsions. Niebuhr would not forget Saint Augustine's warning that the mind may control the body but cannot control itself. Yet in American life few question that freedom is anything but a self-evident truth, eternally subject to rebirth and reaffirmation.

Reinhold Niebuhr was no enemy of human freedom, but he tried to make us aware of the ironies inherent in the concept. Where there is freedom, he observed, there is also power, and where there is power, there is sin and the temptation to sin. Rarely does America see itself solely in terms of power. Instead, we overestimate our dedication to freedom and forget that we are as much creatures of history as its creators. Niebuhr liked to quote Henry Adams's three-word dictum: "Power is poison," and he would cite an observation made by the historian's great-grandfather, John Adams, in a letter to Thomas Jefferson in 1816:

> Power [is] always sincerely, conscientiously *de tres foi* [in very good faith] and believes itself right. Power always thinks it has a great soul, and vast views, beyond the comprehension of the weak; and that it is doing God's service, when it is violating all his laws.[4]

Adams's observation would have perplexed the great anti-Christians of Europe, from Edward Gibbon to Friedrich Nietzsche. It was their view that humankind was weak and submissive. They blamed Christianity, which had shackled power to moralism and celebrated submissive martyrs who would rather lie down before lions than take up the sword. Niebuhr saw history differently. He believed America had a great will to power and that Christianity had too often made excuses for it, dismissing any stirrings of guilt and responsibility. "Power always thinks it has a great soul."

The problem for America was and is pride, the nation's high opinion of its own morality. Pride denies dependency and liberates the self to bend others to its will. Few Americans recognize the sin of pride; our self-confident national character has no place for it. From the transcendentalist Ralph Waldo Emerson to the pragmatist William James, American philosophers have urged their countrymen to practice "self-reliance" and trust the "will to believe."

Niebuhr followed Saint Augustine in seeing the self as the seat of sin, yet he devoted his intellectual life to explaining how love can overcome pride and self-deceit. Moreover, he chastised liberals, urging them to understand that they needed to accept the truth of humanity's Fall so that they could better confront fascism and communism. Gibbon and Nietzsche thought Christians preferred to obey and suffer rather than fight and conquer, and to be sure, there were many liberal Christian pacifists at the outbreak of World War II and the onset of the Cold War. Niebuhr's challenge was to rescue religion from a posture of helplessness and unarmed innocence while avoiding righteousness and arrogance, the signs of sinful pride.

Scholars of various stripes note that Niebuhr treated the Scriptures as symbolic representations of Christianity's "impossible ideal." This is not to say that Niebuhr did not believe in the biblical God, only that he understood the Bible as an authentic mythology containing paradoxical wisdom. Hence, the myth of the Fall clarifies why sin came into the world; the myth of the Creator God helps us conceive of a supreme being as judge and redeemer; and the myth of the Atonement teaches the redeeming power of Jesus on

the cross, the supreme symbol of love and forgiveness.[5] The ultimate paradox of Christianity is that humankind is invited to follow
"the absolutism and perfectionism of Jesus's love ethic," a teaching
that points toward an ultimate perfection that cannot be achieved
in history.[6]

In "Friday's Child" (1958), a poem dedicated to the memory of
the anti-Nazi pastor and martyr Dietrich Bonhoeffer, Niebuhr's
friend W. H. Auden put the dilemma given to us by God:

> He told us we were free to choose . . .
> And must put up with having learned
> All proofs or disproofs that we tender
> Of His existence are returned
> Unopened to the sender.[7]

Two centuries before Niebuhr, the great Puritan theologian Jonathan Edwards upheld the truths of ancient religion by challenging
the advocates of reason.[8] America had fallen under the influence
of John Locke, David Hume, and the eighteenth-century thinkers
of the Scottish Enlightenment, who argued that knowledge comes
through the senses, that "life, liberty, and estates" are the driving
motives of life, and that experience is our only guide. It was left
to Edwards to puncture the pretensions of reason and experience
and to refute a moral philosophy based on self-interest. Edwards
preached that creatures who are finite and imperfect are neither
the best judges of their own interests nor can they comprehend a
perfect and eternal God. Edwards and Niebuhr agreed that God
cannot be known by reason. We may as well give a flashlight to a
blind man.

God's silence prompts the mind to wonder why a supreme being would refuse to reveal its purposes or provide evidence for its
existence? Nietzsche stated the prosecutor's case in *The Dawn of
Day* (1881):

> The Honesty of God—an omniscient and omnipotent God who
> does not even take care that His intentions should be understood

114 • CHAPTER SIX

by his creature—Could He be a God of goodness? A God, who, for thousands of years, has permitted innumerable doubts and scruples to continue unchecked as if they were of no importance in the salvation of mankind, and who, nevertheless, announces the most dreadful consequences for any one who mistakes his truth? Would he not be a cruel god if, being himself in possession of the truth, he could calmly contemplate mankind, in a state of miserable torment, worrying its mind as to what was truth?[9]

Niebuhr could understand Nietzsche's anger at God's inscrutability and his excoriation of Christian meekness. Indeed, in the 1930s America could have used a touch of the "will to power" to stand up to Hitler and Stalin. Nietzsche declared the death of God in order to release humankind from the grip of pity. By contrast, Niebuhr proclaimed Christianity's power in order to sharpen our sense of sin and compel us to do justice to one another.

Niebuhr owes much to modern existential thinkers such as Nietzsche, Søren Kierkegaard, William James, Martin Heidegger, and Max Weber. Their work called a halt to philosophy's search for reasoned explanation and objective truth. Instead of presupposing the presence of what they sought, these modern thinkers treated knowing less as an act of discovery than as a leap of faith. With philosophy at an impasse, Niebuhr could restate the case for religion.

Niebuhr's sense of the unknowable sacrificial God, who asks our love though his purposes are obscure, is akin to the message Herman Melville offered in his profound story "Billy Budd." When the young and innocent sailor Billy Budd impulsively strikes out and kills a lying accuser, his judge, Captain Vere, must condemn him to hang for his crime. Vere is often thought to represent the force of authority and the rule of law, which tragically must prevail over absolute innocence. But what if the story dramatizes religious redemption more than political necessity? "Struck by an angel of God! Yet the angel must hang!" exclaims Captain Vere, while, on the gallows, Billy cries out, "God bless Captain Vere." Christianity offers the forgiveness of sin but can give no reason for the sacrifice of innocence.[10] This riddle, as we have seen, is "the tease of theology."

THE CITY OF MAN

What more can religion show us than that the mind cannot understand what it most wants to know? This question takes us from theology to political philosophy, and the answer in Western thought lands with the force of an arrest warrant. From Machiavelli to Nietzsche, from the early Renaissance to the dawn of modernity, political philosophers warn us that religion will sap our strength, subvert our masculinity, and undo the drive to power, replacing force with conscience. Machiavelli feared for the pious prince who lacked the arts of deception, and Nietzsche scorned Christianity as "the metaphysics of the hangman," who punishes anyone with the nerve to disobey. Immersed in pity, religion urges submission and demands obedience. Christianity is the refuge of the wimp!

With its focus on the origins and ends of life and its emphasis on humility and forgiveness, Christianity might appear to offer no teaching about worldly power. But Niebuhr believed Christianity did have a message for those who are willing to confront evil here and now. It was an unorthodox teaching that surprised the secular liberals and liberal Christians who were Niebuhr's most avid readers.

According to Niebuhr, when Christianity commands us to do good, it demands the impossible. It compels us to aspire to a surrender of selfishness that our human condition rejects. Niebuhr frequently cited Romans 7:19, which describes the dilemma: "For the good that I would I do not: but the evil which I would not, that I do." Niebuhr also denied the possibility that religion can redeem history. He insisted that humanity is fated to endure the "city of man," where alienation persists and corruption prevails: "Where there is history at all there is freedom; and where there is freedom there is sin."[11]

To overcome egoism and pride, Niebuhr observed that Saint Augustine had offered some admirable but dubious advice: We must "commingle" the love of self with the love of God. But the redeeming truths of Augustine's City of God could not do much for a humanity bound by time and space. Augustine defined perfection in history as contemplation of the eternal, and he instructed humanity to aspire to the *civitas dei*, where the law of love banishes the temptations of the flesh. But Niebuhr focused instead on the perils of this world. Man has free will but is enslaved to sin. And while sin is not a necessity, it is natural and universal, a consequence of original sin, humanity's fallen state.[12]

For Niebuhr the promise of Christianity is defined by paradox. Because humanity lives in a world of "contingency and caprice," modern secularism and liberal Christianity attempted to create a basis for moral conduct in terms of the "relatively good and relatively evil." Niebuhr lamented that those holding this view render themselves "partly blind to the total dimension of life and, being untouched by its majesties and tragedies . . . give themselves to the immediate tasks before them." By contrast, prophetic Christianity allows humankind to travel beyond the shadowed valleys of historical time. The Christian can reach the mountain peaks above the "timber line" beyond which life cannot independently sustain itself. The problem here is that Christianity's ethical ideal is an impossible one. We aspire to it while shackled to the lust for power and the passion for possession.[13]

If humankind's love of power was the great problem for Reinhold Niebuhr, it was an untapped potency for Friedrich Nietzsche. In *The Will to Power* the German philosopher asserted, "We do not know how to explain change except as an encroachment of one power on another."[14] Obsessed with the omnipresence of power in the world, Nietzsche repudiated Christianity as a "slave morality."

Today, Reinhold Niebuhr's reputation is undergoing a revival but his ideas are ignored. Alone among modern thinkers, Niebuhr turned to religion for instruction in how to think about power. Unlike those who now celebrate American "Unipower" in a post–Cold War world, where it is thought that American military might can achieve moral ends for liberal democracy's sake,[15] Niebuhr cautioned against identifying power with virtue. It was a conceit of pride, Christianity's fatal sin.

Niebuhr shows us how to think about power. In the best-selling *The God Delusion* (2006), the British scientist Richard Dawkins picks over the traditional "proofs" for God's existence before lambasting religion for inciting bigotry, intolerance, war, and other horrors committed in God's name. Religion's contributions to civilization, from abolitionism and pacifism to relief for the poor and humanitarian assistance to victims of war and famine, go unremarked. God may be a delusion, true enough. But Niebuhr addresses the realities of human affairs and demonstrates that until we consider certain Christian insights about human nature, we can never understand the nature of power in history.

In *The Anti Christ* (1888), Nietzsche offered his understanding of power:

> What is good?—Whatever augments the feeling of power, the will to power, power itself, in man.
>
> What is evil?—Whatever springs from weakness.
>
> What is happiness?—The feeling that power *increases*—that resistance is overcome.[16]

Nietzsche lamented Christianity's success in subduing the instinct for power, an attribute he identified with goodness and happiness. But Nietzsche's account is wrong and his theory is backward. In America, Christianity has failed to subdue power, and while power may be the inextinguishable expression of pride, it is more likely to express a sickness of the soul than the strength of the will. Here the theologian knew better than the philosopher.

In *Treatise on the Gods* (1930), H. L. Mencken, Nietzsche's gleeful promoter, gave voice to American intellectuals of the "lost generation" who discovered, as F. Scott Fitzgerald put it, "all gods dead, all wars fought, all faiths in man shaken." Mencken thought he knew why religion had lost its hold on the modern mind. "The whole Christian system, like every other similar system, goes to pieces upon the problem of evil."[17]

Offering a profoundly new interpretation of Christianity, Reinhold Niebuhr put the pieces back together.

Notes

INTRODUCTION

1. Reinhold Niebuhr, "Pius XI and His Successor," *Nation* (January 30, 1937), in Niebuhr, *Essays in Applied Christianity*, ed. D. B. Robertson (New York: Meridian, 1959), 201–6.

2. Reinhold Niebuhr, *Christianity and Power Politics* (1940; New York: Archon, 1969), 95–105.

3. See Will Herberg, *Judaism and Modern Man: An Interpretation of Jewish Religion* (New York: Atheneum, 1951).

4. Reinhold Niebuhr, "Anti-Semitism," *Radical Religion* 3 (Summer 1938), in Charles C. Brown, *Niebuhr and His Age: Reinhold Niebuhr's Prophetic Role and Legacy* (Harrisburg, PA: Trinity Press International, 2002), 95.

5. John Dewey, "No Matter What Happens—Stay Out," *Common Sense* (March 8, 1939), in *The Later Works of John Dewey, 1925–1953*, ed. Jo Ann Boydston (Carbondale: Southern Illinois University Press, 1988), 14:364.

6. Reinhold Niebuhr, "Utilitarian Christianity and the World Crisis," *Christianity and Crisis* (May 29, 1950), in Niebuhr, *Essays in Applied Christianity*, 95.

7. Peter Beinart, "The Rehabilitation of the Cold War Liberal," *New York Times Sunday Magazine* (April 30, 2006).

8. Reinhold Niebuhr, *The Structure of Nations and Empires* (New York: Charles Scribner's Sons, 1959), 29.

9. See Michael Novak, *The Spirit of Democratic Capitalism* (Lanham, MD: National Book Network, 2000).

10. Friedrich Nietzsche, *The Will to Power*, note 786, cited in Richard Schacht, *Nietzsche* (New York: Routledge, 1983), 450.

11. Christopher Hitchens, *God Is Not Great: How Religion Poisons Everything* (New York: Twelve Books, 2007), 283.

12. Friedrich Nietzsche, *On the Genealogy of Morals*, trans. Walter Kaufman and R. J. Hollingdale (New York: Vintage, 1969), 155.

13. Reinhold Niebuhr, *The Nature and Destiny of Man* (1941,1943; Louisville, KY: Westminster John Knox Press, 1996), 1:97.

CHAPTER ONE

1. Blaise Pascal, *Pensees*, trans. A. J. Kraisheimer (New York: Penguin, 1995), 119 (no. 405).

2. Sidney Hook, "The Moral Vision of Reinhold Niebuhr," in *Pragmatism and the Tragic Sense of Life* (New York: Basic Books, 1974), 184–89.

3. Richard Wightman Fox, *Reinhold Niebuhr: A Biography* (1985; Ithaca: Cornell University Press, 1996), 1–40.

4. Alexis de Tocqueville, *Democracy in America*, trans. George Lawrence, ed. J. P. Mayer (New York: Doubleday Anchor, 1969). See esp. vol.2, part 2, chap. 10; pt. 3, chap.16, 530–32, 612–14.

5. F. Scott Fitzgerald, *The Crack-Up* (1936, New York: New Directions, 1956), 87.

6. Ibid., 79.

7. Reinhold Niebuhr, *An Interpretation of Christian Ethics* (1935; New York: Meridian Books, 1956), 47; Fitzgerald, *Crack-Up*, 69

8. Simone Weil, "The Love of God and Affliction," in *Waiting for God* (New York: Harper Perennial, 2001) 81.

9. Niebuhr, *Nature and Destiny of Man*, 1:182.

10. Ibid. See also Henry Nelson Wieman, "A Religious Naturalist Looks at Reinhold Niebuhr," in *Reinhold Niebuhr: His Religious, Social, and Political Thought*, ed. Charles W. Kegley and Robert W. Bretall (New York: Macmillan, 1956), 334–54.

11. Jerrold Seigel, *The Idea of the Self: Thought and Experience in Western Europe since the Seventeenth Century* (New York: Cambridge University Press, 2005). Seigel's penetrating study concentrates solely on European thinkers. Had he studied American thinkers, the idea of the self would be regarded not only as a philosophical riddle but a religious curse until Ralph Waldo Emerson and John Dewey step forward to save it from original sin.

12. For more on the self and the "sociological turn," see John Patrick Diggins, *The Promise of Pragmatism: Modernism and the Crisis of Knowledge and Authority* (Chicago: University of Chicago Press, 1994), 360–85.

13. Arthur Schlesinger Jr., "Reinhold Niebuhr's Role in American Political Thought and Life," in Kegley and Bretall, *Reinhold Niebuhr*, 124–50.

14. Niebuhr, *Interpretation of Christian Ethics*, 19.

15. Nietzsche, quoted in Schacht, *Nietzsche*, 121. For Marx on religion, see "Toward the Critique of Hegel's Philosophy of Law," in *Writings of the Young Marx on Philosophy and Society*, ed. Loyd Easton and Kurt Guddat (Garden City, NY: Doubleday, 1967), 250.

16. Niebuhr, *Interpretation of Christian Ethics*, 23.

17. Ibid., 24.

18. Niebuhr, "The Sin of Pride," *Detroit Times*, July 6, 1929, quoted in Brown, *Niebuhr and His Age*, 39. I am much indebted to Professor Brown's work.

19. Niebuhr, *Interpretation of Christian Ethics*, 43–62.

20. Ibid., 43–44.

21. Ibid., 62.

22. Ibid., 46–47, quoting Matthew 6:25–26.

23. Ibid., 47, quoting Matthew 19:21.

24. Ibid., 55–56 quoting Matthew 10:39.

25. Ibid., 49.

26. Eastman is quoted in John P. Diggins, *Up from Communism: Conservative Odysseys in American Intellectual History* (New York: Harper & Row, 1975), 17.

27. Niebuhr, *Nature and Destiny of Man*, 1:252–53.

28. Niebuhr, "The Christian Concept of Sin," in *Interpretation of Christian Ethics*, 69, 77.

29. Niebuhr, *Interpretation of Christian Ethics*, 110.

30. Reinhold Niebuhr, "Coherence, Incoherence, and Christian Faith" in *The Essential Reinhold Niebuhr*, ed. Robert McAfee Brown (New Haven: Yale University Press, 1986), 220.

31. Henry Adams, *Mont St. Michel and Chartres*, in *Henry Adams: Novels, Mont St. Michel and Chartres, The Education* (1904; New York: Library of America, 1983), 691.

32. Niebuhr, "Coherence, Incoherence, and Christian Faith," 229.

33. Ibid., 231.

34. Niebuhr, *Nature and Destiny of Man*, 1:16–17.

35. Ibid., 1:23–24.

36. Ibid., 2:187.

37. Ibid.

38. Aquinas is quoted in Leszek Kolakowski, *God Owes Us Nothing: A Brief Remark on Pascal's Religion and the Spirit of Jansenism* (Chicago: University of Chicago Press, 1995), 40–41; F. C. Copleston, *Aquinas* (1956; New York: Penguin Books, 1991), 192.

39. Niebuhr, *Nature and Destiny of Man*, 2:140–43.

40. Ibid., 2:141; Niebuhr, "Coherence, Incoherence, and Christian Faith," 223.

41. Martin Luther, *The Bondage of the Will*, trans. J. I. Packer and O. R. Johnson (Grand Rapids, MI: Fleming H. Revell, 2005), 84.

42. Niebuhr, *Interpretation of Christian Ethics*, 188.

43. Ibid., 189.

44. Fox, *Reinhold Niebuhr*, 32.

45. Reinhold Niebuhr, introduction, in William James, *The Varieties of Religion Experience: A Study in Human Nature* (New York: Simon & Schuster, 2004), v–viii. For James on truth and Santayana on James, see Diggins, *Promise of Pragmatism*, 108–57.

46. Quoted in Jack Miles, *God: A Biography* (New York: Vintage, 1996), 321.

47. Brown, *Niebuhr and His Age*, 30–31.

48. Josef Pieper, *Guide to Thomas Aquinas* (New York: Mentor Omega Book, 1964), 159; Etienne Gilson, *The Christian Philosophy of St. Thomas Aquinas* (Notre Dame, IN: University of Notre Dame Press, 1994), 16.

49. Kolakowski, *God Owes Us Nothing*, 43.

CHAPTER TWO

1. Joseph Wood Krutch, *The Modern Temper* (1929; New York: Harcourt Brace, 1956), 68.

2. Reinhold Niebuhr, *Does Civilization Need Religion?* (New York; Macmillan, 1927), 6.

3. Fox, *Reinhold Niebuhr*, 84.

4. Krutch, *Modern Temper*, 159, 97.

5. Ibid., 15.

6. H. L. Mencken, *Treatise on the Gods* (Baltimore: Johns Hopkins University Press, 1997), 230.

7. Niebuhr, "The Power and Weakness of God," in *Essential Reinhold Niebuhr*, 22; Mencken, *Treatise on the Gods*, 212, 288.

8. Walter Lippmann, *A Preface to Morals*, introduction by John P. Diggins (New York: Transaction Books, 1982), 60.

9. Ibid., 35–36, referring to George Santayana, *The Life of Reason: Reason in Religion* (1905–1906; Amherst, NY: Prometheus Books, 1998), 226.

10. Mencken, introduction, in Friedrich Nietzsche, *The Anti-Christ*, trans. H. L. Mencken (Tucson, AZ: See Sharp Press, 1999), 15. For "recipe for decadence," see *Anti-Christ*, 28 (no. 11), and also Nietzsche, *Ecce Homo* (1908; New York: Penguin, 1991), 61. For "sex, the lust to rule, selfishness," see Schacht, *Nietzsche*, 369.

11. Nietzsche, *Anti-Christ*, 25–26 (nos. 8–9, references to "theological blood"), 23 (no. 5, on Pascal), and 90 (no. 62, on the "worm of sin").

12. Reinhold Niebuhr, *Leaves from the Notebook of a Tamed Cynic* (1929; Louisville, KY: Westminster John Knox Press, 1980), 57.

13. Ibid., 65.

14. Ibid., 118.

15. Reinhold Niebuhr, *Moral Man and Immoral Society: A Study in Ethics and Politics* (Louisville, KY: Westminster John Knox Press, 2001), xxv.

16. Ibid., 35 (possessive instinct), 156 (egotism and vindictiveness), 192 (hopeless romantics).

17. Ibid., 21–22; on necessity, see George Steiner, *The Death of Tragedy* (New York: Oxford, 1961), 342.

18. See John Patrick Diggins, "The Contemporary Critique of the Enlightenment: Its Irrelevance to America and Liberalism," in Neil Jumonville and Kevin Mattson, *Liberalism for a New Century* (Berkeley: University of California Press, 2007), 33–72.

19. Niebuhr, *Moral Man*, 272 (assertions of interest), 266 (less than the best).

20. Martin Luther King Jr., *Why We Can't Wait* (New York: Signet, 2000), 68.

CHAPTER THREE

1. Isaiah Berlin, *Personal Impressions* (New York: Viking Press, 1981), 24.

2. Hannah Arendt, *Eichmann in Jerusalem* (1963, Penguin, 1994), 135–51.

3. Malcolm Cowley and Bernard Smith, eds., *Books That Changed Our Minds* (New York: Kelmscott Editions, 1938), 3–23, 215–35.

4. Niebuhr, *Nature and Destiny of Man*, 2:302–3.

5. G. W. F. Hegel, *Introduction to the Philosophy of History* (Indianapolis: Hackett Publishing, 1988), 73.

6. Paul Schilpp, ed., *The Philosophy of Karl Popper*, part 2 (Lasalle, IL: Open Court, 1974), 1172.

7. Niebuhr, *Nature and Destiny of Man*, 1:9, 20.

8. Ibid., 1:41, 36.

9. Quoted in Claes Ryn, introduction, in Peter Viereck, *Conservatism Revisited* (1949; New Brunswick, NJ: Transaction Publishers, 2005), 21.

10. Peter Viereck, *Metapolitics: From Wagner and the German Romantics to Hitler* (1941; New Brunswick, NJ: Transaction Publishers, 2004), lii.

11. Niebuhr, *Nature and Destiny of Man*, 1:40.

12. Ibid., 1:40, 89.

13. See Diggins, *Promise of Pragmatism*, 386–96.

14. Max Eastman, *Marxism: Is It Science?* (New York: W. W. Norton, 1940), 15.

15. Reinhold Niebuhr, *The Children of Light and the Children of Darkness* (New York: Charles Scribner's Sons, 1944), 9–10.

16. Ibid., 112–13.

17. Ibid., 125.

18. Ibid., xiii.

19. Niebuhr, *Moral Man*, 91.

20. Reinhold Niebuhr, "The Hydrogen Bomb," *Christianity and Society*

124 • *Notes to Pages 64–82*

(Spring 1950), in *Love and Justice: Selections from the Shorter Writings of Reinhold Niebuhr*, ed. D. B. Robertson (Louisville, KY: Westminster John Knox Press, 1957), 237.

21. See Melvyn Leffler, *For the Soul of Mankind: The United States, the Soviet Union, and the Cold War* (New York: Hill and Wang, 2007).

22. Fox, *Reinhold Niebuhr*, 234.

23. Ibid., 235.

24. Sidney Hook, *Out of Step: An Unquiet Life in the 20th Century* (New York: Harper Collins, 1987), 402.

25. Ibid.

26. Niebuhr would later admit that it was a "pedagogical error" to define the persistence of self-regard as *original sin*. He took pains to deny the literal historicity of the Bible story and to reject Augustine's notion that original sin is transmitted through procreation; even though the concept was "historically and symbolically correct," it proved a stumbling block to the modern mind. See Reinhold Niebuhr, *Man's Nature and His Communities* (New York: Charles Scribner's Sons, 1965), 23–24.

27. For the following discussion I have drawn upon the valuable work by Michael Joseph Smith, *Realist Thought: From Weber to Kissinger* (Baton Rouge: Louisiana State University Press, 1986). For some earlier intellectual responses to the cold war, see Diggins, *Up from Communism*.

28. Saint Augustine, *The City of God* (New York: Penguin, 2003), bk.14, chap.13, 571–79.

29. Craig Campbell, "The New Meaning of Modern War in the Thought of Reinhold Niebuhr," *Journal of the History of Ideas* 53 (October–December 1992): 687–701.

30. See John Patrick Diggins, *Ronald Reagan: Fate, Freedom and the Making of History* (New York: W. W. Norton, 2007), 35.

CHAPTER FOUR

1. Howe was sniping at Niebuhr's disciple Will Herberg. See Diggins, *Up from Communism*, 279–80.

2. The criticism by Abraham Heschel and Gustave Weigel is in Kegley and Bretall, *Reinhold Niebuhr*, 368–77, 392–410.

3. Charles Frankel, *The Case for Modern Man* (Boston: Beacon Press, 1955), 43–44, 88–89, 100, 115

4. Morton White, *Social Thought in America: The Revolt against Formalism* (Boston: Beacon Press, 1957), xii.

5. Ibid., 120.

6. Abraham Lincoln, "First Annual Message to Congress" (December 3, 1861), in *Collected Works of Abraham Lincoln* (New Brunswick, NJ: Rutgers University Press, 1953), 5:52.

7. Reinhold Niebuhr, *The Irony of American History* (1952; Chicago: University of Chicago Press, 2008), 171.

8. Ibid., 104.

9. Niebuhr, *Moral Man*, 46.

10. Foucault is quoted in Denise Riley, *Am I That Name? Feminism and the Category of Women in History* (Minneapolis: University of Minnesota Press, 1988), 51.

11. Niebuhr, *Interpretation of Christian Ethics*, 139.

12. Niebuhr, *Children of Light*, 76–77.

13. Niebuhr, *Man's Nature and His Communities*; all quotations on 32–35.

14. Niebuhr, *Nature and Destiny of Man*, 1:239.

15. Hannah Tillich, *From Time to Time* (New York: Stein & Day, 1974).

16. Niebuhr, *Nature and Destiny of Man*, 1:53.

17. Martin Halliwell, *The Constant Dialogue: Reinhold Niebuhr and American Intellectual Culture* (Lanham, MD; Rowman and Littlefield, 2005), 152. For Niebuhr's visits to Erikson, see Fox, *Reinhold Niebuhr*, 260.

18. Reinhold Niebuhr, "The Relations of Christian and Jews in Western Civilization," in *Essential Reinhold Niebuhr*, 188 (on Jews' "civic virtue"). See Diggins, *Up from Communism*, 274–78, for a discussion of Herberg.

19. Reinhold Niebuhr, "Jews after the War," *Nation* (February 21 and 28, 1942), in Robertson, *Love and Justice*, 132–42.

20. David Remnick, "Blood and Sand," *New Yorker* (May 5, 2008), 74.

21. Fox, *Reinhold Niebuhr*, 93–94.

22. Halliwell, *Constant Dialogue*, 225–27; Fox, *Reinhold Niebuhr*, 202.

23. Hannah Arendt, "Reflections on Little Rock," *Dissent* (Winter 1959), in *The Portable Hannah Arendt*, ed. Peter Baehr (New York: Penguin, 2003), 231–46.

24. Fox, *Reinhold Niebuhr*, 238.

25. Niebuhr's review of Erich Fromm's *Man for Himself*, in *Christianity and Society* (Spring 1948), is cited in Paul Ramsey, *Nine Modern Moralists* (Englewood Cliffs, NJ: Prentice-Hall, 1962), 144.

26. Martin Luther King Jr., "I See the Promised Land" (April 3, 1968), in *The Essential Writings and Speeches of Marin Luther King, Jr.*, ed. James M. Washington (San Francisco: Harper Collins, 1981), 279–86.

CHAPTER FIVE

1. Niebuhr, *Irony of American History*, 145–46.

2. Ibid., xxiii–xxv.

3. Ibid., 2.

4. Ibid., 7, 63.

5. Richard Hofstadter, *The American Political Tradition and the Men Who Made It* (New York: Knopf, 1948), viii.

6. See my essays on Boorstin: "Consciousness and Ideology in American His-

tory: The Burden of Daniel J. Boorstin," *American Historical Review* 76 (February 1971): 99–118, and "Daniel J. Boorstin's Approach to American History," *American Quarterly* 23, no. 2 (May 1971): 153–80.

7. Daniel J. Boorstin, *The Genius of American Politics* (Chicago: University of Chicago Press, 1953), 7, 38, 60.

8. Michael Wigglesworth, "A Song of Emptiness" (1657), in *The Puritans: A Sourcebook of their Writings*, ed. Perry Miller and Thomas Johnson (New York: Harper Torchbooks, 1963), 608.

9. John Patrick Diggins, *The Rise and Fall of the American Left* (New York: W. W. Norton, 1992), 196.

10. De Tocqueville, *Democracy in America*, vol. 2, part 2, chap. 9, 528–30. Niebuhr cites the quotation in *Irony of American History*, 53.

11. Louis Hartz, *The Liberal Tradition in America* (New York: Harcourt Brace & World, 1955), 89.

12. Ibid., 125, 264.

13. Niebuhr, *Irony of American History*, 29.

14. Ibid., 33.

15. Ibid., 63.

16. W. H. Auden, "Quartet of Defeated," from his libretto for Benjamin Britten's opera *Paul Bunyan* (1941; London: Faber & Faber, 1988), 32.

17. Henry Adams, *The Education of Henry Adams* (1918; New York: Houghton Mifflin, 2000), xv. Adams was the author of the "editor's preface," which he mischievously attributed to Henry Cabot Lodge.

18. See John Patrick Diggins, *The Lost Soul of American Politics: Virtue, Self-Interest and the Foundations of Liberalism* (Chicago: University of Chicago Press, 1986).

CHAPTER SIX

1. Ursula M Niebuhr, ed., *Remembering Reinhold Niebuhr: Letters of Reinhold Niebuhr and Ursula M. Niebuhr* (New York: Harper Collins, 1991), 182–83.

2. Niebuhr, *Interpretation of Christian Ethics*, 190.

3. Gustave Weigel, SJ, "Authority in Theology," in Kegley and Bretall, *Reinhold Niebuhr*, 367–78.

4. John Adams to Thomas Jefferson, February 2, 1816, in *The Adams-Jefferson Letters*, ed. Lester J. Cappon (Chapel Hill: University of North Carolina Press, 1988), 482; Niebuhr quotes a fragment of the letter in *Irony of American History*, 21.

5. See, for example, Kenneth Durkin, *Reinhold Niebuhr* (London: Geoffrey Chapin, 1989), 107–8.

6. Niebuhr, *Interpretation of Christian Ethics*, 45.

7. W. H. Auden, *Collected Poems*, ed. Edward Mendelson (New York: Random House, 1991), 675.

8. See the valuable study by George M. Marsden, *Jonathan Edwards: A Life* (New Haven, CT: Yale University Press, 2003).

9. Friedrich Nietzsche, *The Dawn of Day*, trans. J. M. Kennedy (New York: Dover, 2007), 90–91.

10. See Diggins, *Lost Soul of American Politics*, 286–96.

11. Niebuhr, *Nature and Destiny of Man*, 2:80.

12. Reinhold Niebuhr, "Augustine's Political Realism," in *Essential Reinhold Niebuhr*, 123–41.

13. Niebuhr, *Interpretation of Christian Ethics*, 97–99.

14. Nietzsche, *Will to Power*, note 689, quoted in Schacht, *Nietzsche*, 216.

15. See Robert Kagan, *Of Paradise and Power: America and Europe in the New World Order* (New York: Knopf, 2003).

16. Nietzsche, *Anti-Christ*, 22.

17. F. Scott Fitzgerald, *This Side of Paradise*, in *Novels and Stories, 1920–1922* (1920; New York: Library of America, 2000), 54; Mencken, *Treatise on the Gods*, 272.

Index

129